LIBERALISM
AND
SOCIAL ACTION

LIBERALISM
AND
SOCIAL ACTION

JOHN
DEWEY

GREAT BOOKS IN PHILOSOPHY

 Prometheus Books

Guilford, Connecticut

Published 2000 by Prometheus Books
4501 Forbes Boulevard, Suite 200
Lanham, Maryland 20706

Library of Congress Cataloging-in-Publication Data

Dewey, John, 1859–1952.
    Liberalism and social action / John Dewey.
        p.   cm. — (Great books in philosophy)
    ISBN 13: 978-1-57392-753-6

    1. Liberalism—History. I. Title. II. Series.
JC574.D48   1999
320.51'.09—dc21   99–39280
                                                      CIP

Distributed by NATIONAL BOOK NETWORK

Great Books in Philosophy Series
(Social and Political Philosophy)

See the back of this volume for a complete list of titles in Prometheus's Great Books in Philosophy and Great Minds series.

JOHN DEWEY was born near Burlington, Vermont, on October 20, 1859. Twenty years later, he graduated from the University of Vermont, after which he taught public school in Pennsylvania and Vermont. Having become interested in philosophical questions while still an undergraduate, Dewey continued his philosophical training at Johns Hopkins University. In 1884 he was awarded a doctorate in philosophy from that institution and soon thereafter he accepted a position in philosophy at the University of Michigan. Except for a one-year appointment as professor of philosophy at the University of Minnesota, Dewey remained at Michigan—serving a five-year term as chairman—until 1894 when he moved with his wife, Alice Chipman, to the University of Chicago and began his tenure as chairman of the philosophy department. It was at Chicago that Dewey received national recognition for his pioneering work in the field of education with the development of his laboratory school in which experimental approaches to teaching were explored. After a falling out with the University of Chicago over the administration of the school, Dewey left in 1904 and accepted a professorship in philosophy at Columbia University.

For the next twenty-six years, Dewey's academic position at Columbia served as a springboard for his many and varied interests—e.g., social questions, politics, education, and public affairs. His national and international reputation found him working with such groups as the American Philosophical Association, the American Association of University Professors (founder and first president), the Teacher's Union, and the American Civil Liberties Union, among others.

Unlike those who consider retirement a time to relax and enjoy the restful pleasures of later life, John Dewey dedicated his remaining years to sorting out the tough social questions facing America and the world. He joined organizations whose goal was to increase public education in the areas of domestic and international politics. One of Dewey's most famous public forums was his participation in the

7

commission that met in Mexico City to inquire into the charges leveled against Leon Trotsky at his Moscow trial. The commission subsequently found Trotsky innocent of the charges. He was also one of several colleagues who publicly defended fellow philosopher Bertrand Russell when Russell was denied a teaching position at the City College of New York because of public criticism of his views on marriage and religion.

In developing his own unique philosophical stance, John Dewey overcame Hegelian idealism to embrace the pragmatic views of William James. Dewey's devotion to free inquiry and the scientific method found him spearheading the intellectual opposition against the belief that absolute knowledge can be attained in a world of variegated circumstances, discoveries, trailblazing research, and advances of all kinds. For Dewey, knowledge is not absolute, immutable, and eternal, but rather relative to the developmental interaction of man with his world as problems arise to present themselves for solution. This scientific approach, which allows one to declare the truth of a claim until—and only until—there is negative evidence sufficient to disconfirm the hypothesis, opens the mind to the need for a democratic approach to problem solving. Without cooperation and a rational tolerance for diverse points of view within a pluralistic community, society has no hope of mature development.

During his ninety-three years, John Dewey authored more than two dozen books and scores of articles in both scholarly and popular publications. He is truly America's foremost philosopher, whose work will influence intellectuals throughout the world for many years to come.

John Dewey died in New York City on June 1, 1952.

Contents

Preface

The chapters that follow were delivered as lectures at the University of Virginia upon the Page-Barbour Foundation. Some passages have been rewritten and the last chapter somewhat enlarged for publication. I wish to express my thanks to the friends, old and new, who did so much to make my stay at the University an enjoyed occasion. I wish also to thank Herbert W. Schneider and Sidney Hook for reading the manuscript and for criticism and comments of which I have freely availed myself. Needless to say, they are not responsible for what I have written. No reference to literature seems to be required, but I am glad to have an opportunity to express my sense of the incalculable worth of the *Encyclopaedia of the Social Sciences* to all students.

There are two requests I should like to make of readers of the volume, not to forestall criticism but that it may be rendered, perhaps, more pertinent. Three lectures do not permit one to say all he thinks, nor even all that he believes that he knows. Omission of topics and themes does not, accordingly, signify that I should have passed them by in a more extended treatment. I particularly regret the enforced omission of reference to the relation of liberalism to international affairs. I should also like to remind readers that not everything can be said in the same breath and that it is necessary to stress first one aspect and then another of the general subject. So I hope that what is said will be taken as a whole and also in comparison and contrast with alternative methods of social action.

New York City,
May, 1935

1.

The History of Liberalism

Liberalism has long been accustomed to onslaughts proceeding from those who oppose social change. It has long been treated as an enemy by those who wish to maintain the *status quo*. But today these attacks are mild in comparison with indictments proceeding from those who want drastic social changes effected in a twinkling of an eye, and who believe that violent overthrow of existing institutions is the right method of effecting the required changes. From current assaults, I select two as typical: "A liberal is one who gives up approval to the grievances of the proletariat, but who at the critical moment invariably runs to cover on the side of the masters of capitalism." Again, a liberal is defined as "one who professes radical opinions in private but who never acts upon them for fear of losing *entrée* into the courts of the mighty and respectable." Such statements might be cited indefinitely. They indicate that, in the minds of many persons, liberalism has fallen between two stools, so that it is conceived as the refuge of those unwilling to take a decided stand in the social conflicts going on. It is called mealy-mouthed, a milk-and-water doctrine and so on.

Popular sentiment, especially in this country, is subject to rapid changes of fashion. It was not a long time ago that liberalism was a term of praise; to be liberal was to be progressive, forward-looking, free from prejudice, characterized by all admirable qualities. I do not think, however, that this particular shift can be dismissed as a mere fluctuation of intellectual fashion. Three of the great nations of Europe have summarily suppressed the civil liberties for which liberalism valiantly strove, and in few countries of the Continent are they maintained with vigor. It is true that none of the nations in question has any long history of devotion to liberal ideals. But the new attacks proceed from those who profess they are concerned to change not to preserve old institutions. It is well known that everything for which liberalism stands is put in peril in times of war. In a world crisis, its ideals and methods are equally challenged; the belief spreads that liberalism flourishes only in times of fair social weather.

It is hardly possible to refrain from asking what liberalism really is; what elements, if any, of permanent value it contains, and how these values shall be maintained and developed in the conditions the world now faces. On my own account, I have raised these questions. I have wanted to find out whether it is possible for a person to continue, honestly and intelligently, to be a liberal, and if the answer be in the affirmative, what kind of liberal faith should be asserted today. Since I do not suppose that I am the only one who has put such questions to himself, I am setting forth the conclusions to which my examination of the problem has led me. If there is danger, on one side, of cowardice and evasion, there is danger on the other side of losing the sense of historic perspective and of yielding precipitately to short-time contemporary currents, abandoning in panic things of enduring and priceless value.

The natural beginning of the inquiry in which we are engaged is consideration of the origin and past development of liberalism. It is to this topic that the present chapter is devoted. The conclusion reached from a brief survey of history, namely, that liberalism has had a chequered career, and that it has meant in practice things so different as to be opposed to one another, might perhaps have been anticipated without prolonged examination of its past. But location and description of the ambiguities that cling to the career of liberalism will be of assistance in the attempt to determine its significance for today and tomorrow.

The use of the words liberal and liberalism to denote a particular social philosophy does not appear to occur earlier than the first decade of the nineteenth century. But the thing to which the words are applied is older. It might be traced back to Greek thought; some of its ideas, especially as to the importance of the free play of intelligence, may be found notably expressed in the funeral oration attributed to Pericles. But for the present purpose it is not necessary to go back of John Locke, the philosopher of the "glorious revolution" of 1688. The outstanding points of Locke's version of liberalism are that governments are instituted to protect the rights that belong to individuals prior to political organization of social relations. These rights are those summed up a century later in the American Declaration of Independence: the rights of life, liberty and the pursuit of happiness. Among the "natural" rights especially emphasized by Locke is that of property, originating, according to him, in the fact that an individual has "mixed" himself, through his labor, with some natural hitherto unappropriated object. This view was directed against levies on property made by rulers without authorization from the representatives of the people. The theory culminated in justifying the right of revolution. Since governments are instituted to protect the natural rights of individuals, they lose claim to obedience when they invade and destroy these rights instead of safeguarding them: a doctrine that well served the alms of our forefathers in their revolt against British rule, and that also found an extended application in the French Revolution of 1789.

The impact of this earlier liberalism is evidently political. Yet one of Locke's greatest interests was to uphold toleration in an age when intolerance was rife, persecution of dissenters in faith almost the rule, and when wars, civil and between nations, had a religious color. In serving the immediate needs of England—and then those of other countries in which it was desired to substitute representative for arbitrary government—it bequeathed to later social thought a rigid doctrine of natural rights inherent in individuals independent of social organization. It gave a directly practical import to the older semi-theological and semi-metaphysical conception of natural law as supreme over positive law and gave a new version of the old idea that natural law is the counterpart of reason, being disclosed by the natural light with which man is endowed.

The whole temper of this philosophy is individualistic in the sense in which individualism is opposed to organized social action. It held to the primacy of the individual over the state not only in time but in moral authority. It defined the individual in terms of liberties of thought and action already possessed by him in some mysterious ready-made fashion, and which it was the sole business of the state to safeguard. Reason was also made an inherent endowment of the individual, expressed in men's moral relations to one another, but not sustained and developed because of these relations. It followed that the great enemy of individual liberty was thought to be government because of its tendency to encroach upon the innate liberties of individuals. Later liberalism inherited this conception of a natural antagonism between ruler and ruled, interpreted as a natural opposition between the individual and organized society. There still lingers in the minds of some the notion that there are two different "spheres" of action and of rightful claims; that of political society and that of the individual, and that in the interest of the latter the former must be as contracted as possible. Not till the second half of the nineteenth century did the idea arise that government might and should be an instrument for securing and extending the liberties of individuals. This later aspect of liberalism is perhaps foreshadowed in the clauses of our Constitution that confer upon Congress power to provide for "public welfare" as well as for public safety.[1]

What has already been said indicates that with Locke the inclusion of the economic factor, property, among natural rights had a political animus. However, Locke at times goes so far as to designate as property everything that is included in "life, liberties and estates"; the individual has property in himself and in his life and activities; property in this broad sense is that which political society should protect. The importance attached to the right of property within the political area was

---

1. Probably in the minds of the framers of the Constitution not much more was contemplated by this clause than the desirability of permitting Congress to make appropriations for roads, rivers and harbors. In subsequent practice, the power has not been used much beyond provision of limited social services for those at an economic disadvantage.

without doubt an influence in the later definitely economic formulation of liberalism. But Locke was interested in property already possessed. A century later industry and commerce were sufficiently advanced in Great Britain so that interest centered in *production* of wealth, rather than in its possession. The conception of labor as the source of right in property was employed not so much to protect property from confiscation by the ruler (that right was practically secure in England) as to urge and justify freedom in the use and investment of capital and the right of laborers to move about and seek new modes of employment—claims denied by the common law that came down from semi-feudal conditions. The earlier economic conception may fairly be called static; it was concerned with possessions and estates. The newer economic conception was dynamic. It was concerned with release of productivity and exchange from a cumbrous complex of restrictions that had the force of law. The enemy was no longer the arbitrary special action of rulers. It was the whole system of common law and judicial practice in its adverse bearing upon freedom of labor, investment and exchange.

The transformation of earlier liberalism that took place because of this new interest is so tremendous that its story must be told in some detail. The concern for liberty and for the individual, which was the basis of Lockeian liberalism, persisted; otherwise the newer theory would not have been liberalism. But liberty was given a very different practical meaning. In the end, the effect was to subordinate political to economic activity; to connect natural laws with the laws of production and exchange, and to give a radically new significance to the earlier conception of reason. The name of Adam Smith is indissolubly connected with initiation of this transformation.

Although he was far from being an unqualified adherent of the idea of *laissez faire*, he held that the activity of individuals, freed as far as possible from political restriction, is the chief source of social welfare and the ultimate spring of social progress. He held that there is a "natural" or native tendency in every individual to better each his own estate through putting forth effort (labor) to satisfy his natural wants. Social welfare is promoted because the cumulative, but undesigned and unplanned, effect of the convergence of a multitude of individual efforts is to increase the commodities and services put at the disposal of men collectively, of society. This increase of goods and services creates new wants and leads to putting forth new modes of productive energy. There is not only a native impulse to exchange, to "truck," but individuals are released by the processes of exchange from the necessity for labor in order to satisfy all of the individual's own wants; through division of labor, productivity is enormously increased. Free economic processes thus bring about an endless spiral of ever increasing change, and through the guidance of an "invisible hand" (the equivalent of the doctrine of preestablished harmony so dear to the eighteenth century) the efforts of individuals for personal advancement and personal gain accrue to the benefit of society, and create a continuously closer knit interdependence of interests.

The ideas and ideals of the new political economy were congruous with the increase of industrial activity that was marked in England even before the invention of the steam engine. They spread rapidly. Their power was furthered when the great industrial and commercial expansion of England ensued in the wake of the substitution of mechanical for human energy, first in textiles and then in other occupations.

Under the influence of the industrial revolution the old argument against political action as a social agency assumed a new form. Such action was not only an invasion of individual liberty but it was in effect a conspiracy against the causes that bring about social progress. The Lockeian idea of natural laws took on a much more concrete, a more directly practical, meaning. Natural law was still regarded as something more fundamental than man-made law, which by comparison is artificial. But natural laws lost their remote moral meaning. They were identified with the laws of free industrial production and free commercial exchange. Adam Smith, however, did not originate this latter idea. He took it over from the French physiocrats, who, as the name implies, believed in rule of social relations by natural law and who identified natural with economic law.

France was an agricultural country, and the economy of the physiocrats was conceived and formulated in the interest of agriculture and mining. Land, according to them, is the source of all wealth; from it comes ultimately all genuinely productive force. Industry, as distinct from agriculture, merely reshapes what nature provides. The movement was essentially a protest against governmental measures that were impoverishing the agriculturalist and that enriched idle parasites. But its underlying philosophy was the idea that economic laws are the true natural laws while other laws are artificial and hence to be limited in scope as far as possible. In an ideal society political organization will be modeled upon the economic pattern set by nature. *Ex natura, jus.*

Locke had taught that labor, not land, is the source of wealth, and England was passing from an agrarian to an industrialized community. The French doctrine in its own form did not fit into the English scene. But there was no great obstacle against translating the underlying ideal of the identity of natural law with economic law into a form suited to the needs of an industrial community. The shift from land to labor (the expenditure of energy for the satisfaction of wants) required only, from the side of the philosophy of economics, that attention be centered upon human nature, rather than upon physical nature. Psychological laws, based on human nature, are as truly natural as are any laws based on land and physical nature. Land is itself productive only under the influence of the labor put forth in satisfaction of intrinsic human wants. Adam Smith was not himself especially interested in elaborating a formulation of laws in terms of human nature. But he explicitly fell back upon one natural human tendency, sympathy, to find the basis for morals, and he used other natural impulses, the instincts to better one's condition and to exchange, to give the foundation of economic theory. The laws of the operations of these natural tendencies, when they are freed from artificial restraints, are the natural laws governing men in their relations to one another. In individuals, the exercise of sympathy in accordance with reason (that is, in Smith's conception, from the standpoint of an impartial spectator) is the norm of virtuous action. But government cannot appeal to sympathy. The only measures it can employ affect the motive of self-interest. It makes this appeal most effectively when it acts so as to protect individuals in the exercise of their natural self-interest. These ideas, implicit in Smith, were made explicit by his successors: in part by the classical school of economists and in part by Bentham and the Mills, father and son. For a considerable period these two schools worked hand in hand.

Economists developed the principle of the free economic

activity of individuals; since this freedom was identified with absence of governmental action, conceived as an interference with natural liberty, the result was the formulation of *laissez faire* liberalism. Bentham carried the same conception, though from a different point of view, into a vigorous movement for reform of the common law and judicial procedure by means of legislative action. The Mills developed the psychological and logical foundation implicit in the theories of the economists and of Bentham.

I begin with Bentham. The existing legal system was intimately bound up with a political system based upon the predominance of the great landed proprietors through the rotten borough system. The operation of the new industrial forces in both production and exchange was checked and deflected at almost every point by a mass of customs that formed the core of common law. Bentham approached the situation not from the standpoint of individual liberty but from the standpoint of the effect of these restrictions upon the happiness enjoyed by individuals. Every restriction upon liberty is *ipso facto* a source of pain and a limitation of a pleasure that might otherwise be enjoyed. Hence the effect was the same in the two doctrines as far as the rightful province of governmental action is concerned. Bentham's assault was aimed directly, not indirectly, like the theory of the economists, upon everything in existing law and judicial procedure that inflicted unnecessary pain and that limited the acquisition of pleasures by individuals. Moreover, his psychology converted the impulse to improve one's condition, upon which Adam Smith had built, into the doctrine that desire for pleasure and aversion to pain are the sole forces that govern human action. The psychological theory implicit in the idea of industry and exchange controlled by desire for gain was then worked out upon the political and legal side. Moreover, the constant expansion of manufacturing and trade put the force of a powerful class interest behind the new version of liberalism. This statement does not imply that the intellectual leaders of the new liberalism were themselves moved by hope of material gain. On the contrary, they formed a group animated by a strikingly unselfish spirit, in contrast with their professed theories. Their very detachment from the immediate interests of the market place liberated them from the narrowness and shortsightedness that marked the trading class—a class that John Stuart Mill adverted to with even more bitterness than did Adam Smith. This emancipation enabled them to detect and make articulate the nascent movements of their time—a function that defines the genuine work of the intellectual class at any period. But they might have been as voices crying in the wilderness if what they taught had not coincided with the interests of a class that was constantly rising in prestige and power.

According to Bentham, the criterion of all law and of every administrative effort is its effect upon the sum of happiness enjoyed by the greatest possible number. In calculating this sum, every individual is to count as one and only as one. The mere formulation of the doctrine was an attack upon every inequality of status that had the sanction of law. In effect, it made the well-being of the individual the norm of political action in every area in which it operates. In effect, though not wholly in Bentham's express apprehension, it transferred attention from the well-being already possessed by individuals to one they might attain if there were a radical change in social institutions. For existing institutions enabled a small number of individuals to enjoy their pleasures at the cost of the misery of a much greater number. While Bentham himself conceived that the changes to be made in legal and political institutions were mainly negative, such as abolition of abuses, corruptions and inequalities, nevertheless (as we shall see later) there was nothing in his fundamental doctrine that stood in the way of using the power of government to create, constructively and positively, new institutions if and when it should appear that the latter would contribute more effectively to the well-being of individuals.

Bentham's best known work is entitled *Principles of Morals and Legislation*. In his actual treatment "morals and legislation" form a single term. It was the morals *of* legislation, of political action generally, with which he occupied himself, his standard being the simple one of determination of its effect upon the greatest possible happiness of the greatest possible number. He labored incessantly to expose the abuses of the existing legal system and its application in judicial procedure, civil and criminal, and in administration. He attacked these abuses, in his various works, in detail, one by one. But his attacks were cumulative in effect since he applied a single principle in his detailed criticism. He was, we may say, the first great muck-raker in the field of law. But he was more than that. Wherever he saw a defect, he proposed a remedy. He was an inventor in law and administration, as much so as any contemporary in mechanical production. He said of himself that his ambition was to "extend the experimental method of reasoning from the physical branch to the moral"—meaning, in common with English thought of the eighteenth century, by the moral the human. He also compared his own work with what physicists and chemists were doing in their fields in invention of appliances and processes that increase human welfare. That is, he did not limit his method to mere reasoning; the latter occurred only for the sake of instituting changes in actual practice. History shows no mind more fertile than his invention of legal and administrative devices. Of him and his school, Graham Wallas said, "The fact that the fall from power of the British aristocracy in 1832 led neither to social revolution or administrative chaos at home, nor to the break up of the new British Empire abroad was largely due to the political expedients—local government reform, open competition in the civil service, scientific health and police administration, colonial self-government, Indian administrative reform—which Bentham's disciples either found in his writings, or developed, after his death, by his methods."[2]

The work of Bentham, in spite of fundamental defects in his underlying theory of human nature, is a demonstration that liberalism is not compelled by anything in its own nature to be impotent save for minor reforms. Bentham's influence is proof that liberalism can be a power in bringing about radical social changes:—provided it combine capacity for bold and comprehensive social invention with detailed study of particulars and with courage in action. The history of the legal and administrative changes in Great Britain during the first half of the nineteenth century is chiefly the history of Bentham and his school. I think there is something significant for the liberalism of today and tomorrow to be found in the fact that his group did not consist in any large measure of politicians, legislators or public officials. On the American principle of "Let George do it," liberals in this country are given to supposing and hoping that some Administration when in power will take the lead in

2. Article on Bentham in the *Encyclopaedia of the Social Sciences*, Vol. 11, p. 519.

formulating and executing liberal policies. I know of nothing in history that justifies the belief and hope. A liberal program has to be developed, and in a good deal of particularity, outside of the immediate realm of governmental action and enforced upon public attention, before direct political action of a thoroughgoing liberal sort will follow. This is one lesson we have to learn from early nineteenth-century liberalism. Without a background of informed political intelligence, direct action in behalf of professed liberal ends may end in development of political irresponsibility.

Bentham's theory led him to the view that all organized action is to be judged by its consequences, consequences that take effect in the lives of individuals. His psychology was rather rudimentary. It made him conceive of consequences as being atomic units of pleasures and pains that can be algebraically summed up. It is to this aspect of his doctrines that later writers, especially moralists, have chiefly devoted their critical attention. But this particular aspect of his theory, if we view it in the perspective of history, is an adventitious accretion. His enduring idea is that customs, institutions, laws, social arrangements are to be judged on the basis of their consequences as these come home to the individuals that compose society. Because of his emphasis upon consequences, he made short work of the tenets of both of the two schools that had dominated, before his day, English political thought. He brushed aside, almost contemptuously, the conservative school that found the source of social wisdom in the customs and precedents of the past. This school has its counterpart in those empiricists of the present day who attack every measure and policy that is new and innovating on the ground that it does not have the sanction of experience, when what they really mean by "experience" is patterns of mind that were formed in a past that no longer exists.

But Bentham was equally aggressive in assault upon that aspect of earlier liberalism which was based upon the conception of inherent natural rights—following in this respect a clew given by David Hume. Natural rights and natural liberties exist only in the kingdom of mythological social zoology. Men do not obey laws because they think these laws are in accord with a scheme of natural rights. They obey because they believe, rightly or wrongly, that the consequences of obeying are upon the whole better than the consequences of disobeying. If the consequences of existing rule become too intolerable, they revolt. An enlightened self-interest will induce a ruler not to push too far the patience of subjects. The enlightened self-interest of citizens will lead them to obtain by peaceful means, as far as possible, the changes that will effect a distribution of political power and the publicity that will lead political authorities to work for rather than against the interests of the people—a situation which Bentham thought was realized by government that is representative and based upon popular suffrage. But in any case, not natural rights but consequences in the lives of individuals are the criterion and measure of policy and judgment.

Because the liberalism of the economists and the Benthamites was adapted to contemporary conditions in Great Britain, the influence of the liberalism of the school of Locke waned. By 1820 it was practically extinct. Its influence lasted much longer in the United States. We had no Bentham and it is doubtful whether he would have had much influence if he had appeared. Except for movements in codification of law, it is hard to find traces of the influence of Bentham in this country. As was intimated earlier, the philosophy of Locke bore much the same relation to the American revolt of the colonies that it had to the British revolution of almost a century earlier. Up to, say, the time of the Civil War, the United States were predominantly agrarian. As they became industrialized, the philosophy of liberty of individuals, expressed especially in freedom of contract, provided the doctrine needed by those who controlled the economic system. It was freely employed by the courts in declaring unconstitutional legislation that limited this freedom. The ideas of Locke embodied in the Declaration of Independence were congenial to our pioneer conditions that gave individuals the opportunity to carve their own careers. Political action was lightly thought of by those who lived in frontier conditions. A political career was very largely annexed as an adjunct to the action of individuals in carving their own careers. The gospel of self-help and private initiative was practiced so spontaneously that it needed no special intellectual support. Finally, there was no background of feudalism to give special leverage to the Benthamite system of legal and administrative reform.

The United States lagged more than a generation behind Great Britain in promotion of social legislation. Justice Holmes found it necessary to remind his fellow justices that, after all, the *Social Statics* of Herbert Spencer had not been enacted into the American Constitution. Great Britain, largely under Benthamite influence, built up an ordered civil service independent of political party control. With us, political emoluments, like economic pecuniary rewards, went to the most enterprising competitor; to the victor belong the spoils. The principle of the greatest good to the greatest number tended to establish in Great Britain the supremacy of national over local interests. The political history of the United States is largely a record of domination by regional interests. Our fervor in law-making might be allied to Bentham's principle of the "omnicompetence" of the legislative body. But we have never taken very seriously the laws we make, while there has been little comparable in our history to the importance attached to administration by the English utilitarian school.

I have mentioned two schools of liberalism in Great Britain, that of the economists and of the utilitarians. At first they walked the same path. The later history of liberalism in that country is largely a matter of a growing divergence, and finally of an open split. While Bentham personally was on the side of the classical economists, his principle of judgment by consequences lends itself to opposite application. Bentham himself urged a great extension of public education and of action in behalf of public health. When he disallowed the doctrine of inalienable individual natural rights, he removed, as far as theory is concerned, the obstacle to positive action by the state whenever it can be shown that the general well-being will be promoted by such action. Dicey in his *Law and Opinion in England* has shown that collectivist legislative policies gained in force for at least a generation after the sixties. It was stimulated, naturally, by the reform bills that greatly broadened the basis of suffrage. The use of scientific method, even if sporadic and feeble, encouraged study of actual consequences and promoted the formation of legislative policies designed to improve the consequences brought about by existing institutions. At all events, in connection with Benthamite influence, it greatly weakened the notion that Reason is a remote majestic power that discloses ultimate truths. It tended to render it an agency in investigation of concrete situations and in projection of measures for their betterment.

I would not, however, give the impression that the trend

away from individualistic to collectivistic liberalism was the direct effect of utilitarianism. On the contrary, social legislation was fostered primarily by Tories, who, traditionally, had no love for the industrialist class. Benthamite liberalism was not the source of factory laws, laws for the protection of child and women, prevention of their labor in mines, workmen's compensation acts, employers' liability laws, reduction of hours of labor, the dole, and a labor code. All of these measures went contrary to the idea of liberty of contract fostered by *laissez faire* liberalism. Humanitarianism, in alliance with evangelical piety and with romanticism, gave chief support, from the intellectual and emotional side, to these measures, as the Tory party was their chief political agent. No account of the rise of humanitarian sentiment as a force in creation of the new regulations of industry would be adequate that did not include the names of religious leaders drawn from both dissenters and the Established Church. Such names as Wilberforce, Clarkson, Zachary Macaulay, Elizabeth Fry, Hannah More, as well as Lord Shaftesbury, come to mind. The trades unions were gaining power and there was an active socialist movement, as represented by Robert Owen. But in spite of, or along with, such movements, we have to remember that liberalism is associated with generosity of outlook as well as with liberty of belief and action. Gradually a change came over the spirit and meaning of liberalism. It came surely, if gradually, to be disassociated from the *laissez faire* creed and to be associated with the use of governmental action for aid to those at economic disadvantage and for alleviation of their conditions. In this country, save for a small band of adherents to earlier liberalism, ideas and policies of this general type have virtually come to define the meaning of liberal faith. American liberalism as illustrated in the political progressivism of the early present century has so little in common with British liberalism of the first part of the last century that it stands in opposition to it.

The influence of romanticism, as exemplified in different ways by Coleridge, Wordsworth, Carlyle and Ruskin, is worthy of especial note. These men were politically allied as a rule with the Tory party, if not actively, at least in sympathy. The romanticists were all of them vigorous opponents of the consequences of the industrialization of England, and directed their assaults at the economists and Benthamites whom they held largely responsible for these consequences. As against dependence upon uncoordinated individual activities, Coleridge emphasized the significance of enduring institutions. They, according to him, are the means by which men are held together in concord of mind and purpose, the only real social bond. They are the force by which human relations are kept from disintegrating into an aggregate of unconnected and conflicting atoms. His work and that of his followers was a powerful counterpoise to the anti-historic quality of the Benthamite school. The leading scientific interest of the nineteenth century came to be history, including evolution within the scope of history. Coleridge was no historian; he had no great interest in historical facts. But his sense of the mission of great historic institutions was profound. Wordsworth preached the gospel of return to nature, of nature expressed in rivers, dales and mountains and in the souls of simple folk. Implicitly and often explicitly he attacked industrialization as the great foe of nature, without and within. Carlyle carried on a constant battle against utilitarianism and the existing socio-economic order, which he summed up in a single phrase as "anarchy plus a constable." He called for a régime of social authority to enforce social ties. Ruskin preached the social importance of art and joined to it a denunciation of the entire reigning system of economics, theoretical and practical. The esthetic socialists of the school of William Morris carried his teachings home to the popular mind.

The romantic movement profoundly affected some who had grown up in the straitest sect of *laissez faire* liberalism. The intellectual career of John Stuart Mill was a valiant if unsuccessful struggle to reconcile the doctrines he derived, almost in infancy, from his father with a feeling of their hollowness when compared with the values of poetry, of enduring historic institutions, and of the inner life, as portrayed by the romanticists. He was keenly sensitive to the brutality of life about him and its low intellectual level, and saw the relation between these two traits. At one time, he even went so far as to say that he looked forward to the coming of an age "when the division of the produce of labour . . . will be made by concert on an acknowledged principle of justice." He asserted that existing institutions were merely provisional, and that the "laws" governing the distribution of wealth are not social but of man's contrivance and are man's to change. A long distance lies between the philosophy embodied in such sayings and his earlier assertion that "the sole end for which mankind are warranted, individually or collectively, in interfering with the freedom of action of any person is self-protection." The romantic school was the chief influence in effecting the change.

There was in addition another intellectual force at work in changing the earlier liberalism, which openly professed liberal aims while at the same time attacking earlier liberalism. The name of Thomas Hill Green is not widely known outside of technical philosophical circles. But he was the leader in introducing into England, in coherent formulation, the organic idealism that originated in Germany—and that originated there largely in reaction against the basic philosophy of individualistic liberalism and individualistic empiricism. John Mill himself was greatly troubled by the consequences that followed from the psychological doctrine of associationalism. Mental bonds in belief and purpose which are the product of external associations can easily be broken when circumstances change. The moral and social consequence is a threatened destruction of all stable bases of belief and social relationship. Green and his followers exposed this weakness in all phases of the atomistic philosophy that had developed under the alleged empiricism of the earlier liberal school. They criticized piece by piece almost every item of the theory of mind, knowledge and society that had grown out of the teachings of Locke. They asserted that *relations* constitute the reality of nature, of mind and of society. But Green and his followers remained faithful, as the romantic school did not, to the ideals of liberalism; the conceptions of a common good as the measure of political organization and policy, of liberty as the most precious trait and very seal of individuality, of the claim of every individual to the full development of his capacities. They strove to provide unshakeable objective foundations in the very structure of things for these moral claims, instead of basing them upon the sandy ground of the feelings of isolated human beings. For the relations that constitute the essential nature of things are, according to them, the expression of an objective Reason and Spirit that sustains nature and the human mind.

The idealistic philosophy taught that men are held together by the relations that proceed from and that manifest an ultimate cosmic mind. It followed that the basis of society and the state is shared intelligence and purpose, not force nor

yet self-interest. The state is a moral organism, of which government is one organ. Only by participating in the common
intelligence and sharing in the common purpose as it works for
the common good can individual human beings realize their
true individualities and become truly free. The state is but one
organ among many of the Spirit and Will that holds all things
together and that makes human beings members of one
another. It does not originate the moral claim of individuals to
the full realization of their potentialities as vehicles of objective
thought and purpose. Moreover, the motives it can directly
appeal to are not of the highest kind. But it is the business of
the state to protect all forms and to promote all modes of
human association in which the moral claims of the members
of society are embodied and which serve as the means of voluntary self-realization. Its business is negatively to remove the
obstacles that stand in the way of individuals coming to con-
sciousness of themselves for what they are, and positively to
promote the cause of public education. Unless the state does
this work it is no state. These philosophical liberals pointed out
the restrictions, economic and political, which prevent many,
probably the majority, of individuals from the voluntary intelligent action by which they may become what they are capable of becoming. The teachings of this new liberal school
affected the thoughts and actions of multitudes who did not
trouble themselves to understand the philosophical doctrine
that underlay it. They served to break down the idea that freedom is something that individuals have as a ready-made possession, and to instill the idea that it is something to be
achieved, while the possibility of the achievement was shown
to be conditioned by the institutional medium in which an
individual lives. These new liberals fostered the idea that the

state has the responsibility for creating institutions under which individuals can effectively realize the potentialities that are theirs.

Thus from various sources and under various influences there developed an inner split in liberalism. This cleft is one cause of the ambiguity from which liberalism still suffers and which explains a growing impotency. There are still those who call themselves liberals who define liberalism in terms of the old opposition between the province of organized social action and the province of purely individual initiative and effort. In the name of liberalism they are jealous of every extension of governmental activity. They may grudgingly concede the need of special measures of protection and alleviation undertaken by the state at times of great social stress, but they are the confirmed enemies of social legislation (even prohibition of child labor), as standing measures of political policy. Wittingly or unwittingly, they still provide the intellectual system of apologetics for the existing economic régime, which they strangely, it would seem ironically, uphold as a régime of individual liberty for all.

But the majority who call themselves liberals today are committed to the principle that organized society must use its powers to establish the conditions under which the mass of individuals can possess actual as distinct from merely legal liberty. They define their liberalism in the concrete in terms of a program of measures moving toward this end. They believe that the conception of the state which limits the activities of the latter to keeping order as between individuals and to securing redress for one person when another person infringes the liberty existing law has given him, is in effect simply a justification of the brutalities and inequities of the existing order.

Because of this internal division within liberalism its later history is wavering and confused. The inheritance of the past still causes many liberals, who believe in a generous use of the powers of organized society to change the terms on which human beings associate together, to stop short with merely protective and alleviatory measures—a fact that partly explains why another school always refers to "reform" with scorn. It will be the object of the next chapter to portray the crisis in liberalism, the *impasse* in which it now almost finds itself, and through criticism of the deficiencies of earlier liberalism to suggest the way in which liberalism may resolve the crisis, and emerge as a compact, aggressive force.

2.

The Crisis in Liberalism

The net effect of the struggle of early liberals to emancipate individuals from restrictions imposed upon them by the inherited type of social organization was to pose a problem, that of a new social organization. The ideas of liberals set forth in the first third of the nineteenth century were potent in criticism and in analysis. They released forces that had been held in check. But analysis is not construction, and release of force does not of itself give direction to the force that is set free. Victorian optimism concealed for a time the crisis at which liberalism had arrived. But when that optimism vanished amid the conflict of nations, classes and races characteristic of the latter part of the nineteenth century—a conflict that has grown more intense with the passing years—the crisis could no longer be covered up. The beliefs and methods of earlier liberalism were ineffective when faced with the problems of social organization and integration. Their inadequacy is a large part of belief now so current that all liberalism is an outmoded doctrine. At the same time, insecurity and uncertainty in belief and purpose

37

are powerful factors in generating dogmatic faiths that are profoundly hostile to everything to which liberalism in any possible formulation is devoted.

In a longer treatment, the crisis could be depicted in terms of the career of John Stuart Mill, during a period when the full force of the crisis was not yet clearly manifest. He records in his *Autobiography* that, as early as 1826, he asked himself this question: "Suppose that all your objects in life were realized: that all the changes in institutions and opinions which you are looking forward to, could be completely effected at this very instant: would this be a great joy and happiness to you?" His answer was negative. The struggle for liberation had given him the satisfaction that comes from active struggle. But the prospect of the goal attained presented him with a scene in which something unqualifiedly necessary for the good life was lacking. He found something profoundly empty in the spectacle he imaginatively faced. Doubtless physical causes had something to do with his growing doubt as to whether life would be worth living were the goal of his ambitious realized; sensitive youth often undergoes such crises. But he also felt that there was something inherently superficial in the philosophy of Bentham and his father. This philosophy now seemed to him to touch only the externals of life, but not its inner springs of personal sustenance and growth. I think it a fair paraphrase to say that he found himself faced with only intellectual abstractions. Criticism has made us familiar with the abstraction known as the economic man. The utilitarians added the abstraction of the legal and political man. But somehow they had failed to touch man himself. Mill first found relief in the fine arts, especially poetry, as a medium for the cultivation of the feelings, and reacted against Benthamism as exclusively intellectualistic, a theory that identified man with a reckoning machine. Then under the influence of Coleridge and his disciples he learned that institutions and traditions are indispensable to the nurture of what is deepest and most worthy in human life. Acquaintance with Comte's philosophy of a future society based on the organization of science gave him a new end for which to strive, the institution of a kind of social organization in which there should be some central spiritual authority.

The life-long struggle of Mill to reconcile these ideas with those which were deeply graven in his being by his earlier Benthamism concern us here only as a symbol of the enduring crisis of belief and action brought about in liberalism itself when the need arose for uniting earlier ideas of freedom with an insistent demand for social organization, that is, for constructive synthesis in the realm of thought and social institutions. The problem of achieving freedom was immeasurably widened and deepened. It did not now present itself as a conflict between government and the liberty of individuals in matters of conscience and economic action, but as a problem of establishing an entire social order, possessed of a spiritual authority that would nurture and direct the inner as well as the outer life of individuals. The problem of science was no longer merely technological applications for increase of material productivity, but imbuing the minds of individuals with the spirit of reasonableness, fostered by social organization and contributing to its development. The problem of democracy was seen to be not solved, hardly more than externally touched, by the establishment of universal suffrage and representative government. As Havelock Ellis has said, "We see now that the vote and the ballot-box do not make the voter free from even external pressure; and, which is of much more consequence, they do not necessarily free him from his own slavish instincts." The problem of democracy becomes the problem of that form of social organization, extending to all the areas and ways of living, in which the powers of individuals shall not be merely released from mechanical external constraint but shall be fed, sustained and directed. Such an organization demands much more of education than general schooling, which without a renewal of the springs of purpose and desire becomes a new mode of mechanization and formalization, as hostile to liberty as ever was governmental constraint. It demands of science much more than external technical application—which again leads to mechanization of life and results in a new kind of enslavement. It demands that the method of inquiry, of discrimination, of test by verifiable consequences, be naturalized in all the matters, of large and of detailed scope, that arise for judgment.

The demand for a form of social organization that should include economic activities but yet should convert them into servants of the development of the higher capacities of individuals, is one that earlier liberalism did not meet. If we strip its creed from adventitious elements, there are, however, enduring values for which earlier liberalism stood. These values are liberty, the development of the inherent capacities of individuals made possible through liberty, and the central role of free intelligence in inquiry, discussion and expression. But elements that were adventitious to these values colored every one of these ideals in ways that rendered them either impotent or perverse when the new problem of social organization arose.

Before considering the three values, it is advisable to note one adventitious idea that played a large role in the later incapacitation of liberalism. The earlier liberals lacked historic sense and interest. For a while this lack had an immediate pragmatic value. It gave liberals a powerful weapon in their fight with reactionaries. For it enabled them to undercut the appeal to origin, precedent and past history by which the opponents of social change gave sacrosanct quality to existing inequities and abuses. But disregard of history took its revenge. It blinded the eyes of liberals to the fact that their own special interpretations of liberty, individuality and intelligence were themselves historically conditioned, and were relevant only to their own time. They put forward their ideas as immutable truths good at all times and places; they had no idea of historic relativity, either in general or in its application to themselves.

When their ideas and plans were projected they were an attack upon the interests that were vested in established institutions and that had the sanction of custom. The new forces for which liberals sought an entrance were incipient; the *status quo* was arrayed against their release. By the middle of the nineteenth century the contemporary scene had radically altered. The economic and political changes for which they strove were so largely accomplished that they had become in turn the vested interest, and their doctrines, especially in the form of *laissez faire* liberalism, now provided the intellectual justification of the *status quo*. This creed is still powerful in this country. The earlier doctrine of "natural rights," superior to legislative action, has been given a definitely economic meaning by the courts, and used by judges to destroy social legislation passed in the interest of a real, instead of purely formal, liberty of contract. Under the caption of "rugged individualism" it inveighs against all new social policies. Beneficiaries of the established economic régime band themselves together in what they call Liberty Leagues to perpetuate the harsh regimentation of millions of their fellows. I do not imply that resistance to change would not have appeared if it had not been for the doctrines of earlier liberals. But had the early liberals appreciated the historic relativity of their own interpretation of the meaning of liberty, the later resistance would certainly have been deprived of its chief intellectual and moral support. The tragedy is that although these liberals were the sworn foes of political absolutism, they were themselves absolutists in the social creed they formulated.

This statement does not mean, of course, that they were opposed to social change; the opposite is evidently the case. But it does mean they held that beneficial social change can come about in but one way, the way of private economic enterprise, socially undirected, based upon and resulting in the sanctity of private property—that is to say, freedom from social control. So today those who profess the earlier type of liberalism ascribe to this factor all social betterment that has occurred; such as the increase in productivity and improved standards of living. The liberals did not try to prevent change, but they did try to limit its course to a single channel and to immobilize the channel.

If the early liberals had put forth their special interpretation of liberty as something subject to historic relativity they would not have frozen it into a doctrine to be applied at all times under all social circumstances. Specifically, they would have recognized that effective liberty is a function of the social conditions existing at any time. If they had done this, they would have known that as economic relations became dominantly controlling forces in setting the pattern of human relations, the necessity of liberty for individuals which they proclaimed will require social control of economic forces in the interest of the great mass of individuals. Because the liberals failed to make a distinction between purely formal or legal liberty and effective liberty of thought and action, the history of the last one hundred years is the history of non-fulfillment of their predictions. It was prophesied that a régime of economic liberty would bring about interdependence among nations and consequently peace. The actual scene has been marked by wars of increasing scope and destructiveness. Even Karl Marx shared the idea that the new economic forces would destroy economic nationalism and usher in an era of internationalism. The display of exacerbated nationalism now characterizing the world is a sufficient comment. Struggle for raw materials and markets in backward countries, combined with foreign financial control of their domestic industrial development, has been accompanied by all kinds of devices to prevent access of other advanced nations to the national market-place.

The basic doctrine of early economic liberals was that the régime of economic liberty as they conceived it, would almost automatically direct production through competition into channels that would provide, as effectively as possible, socially needed commodities and services. Desire for personal gain early learned that it could better further the satisfaction of that desire by stifling competition and substituting great combinations of noncompeting capital. The liberals supposed the motive of individual self-interest would so release productive energies as to produce ever-increasing abundance. They overlooked the fact that in many cases personal profit can be better served by maintaining artificial scarcity and by what Veblen called systematic sabotage of production. Above all, in identifying the extension of liberty in all of its modes with extension of their particular brand of economic liberty, they completely failed to anticipate the bearing of private control of the means of production and distribution upon the effective liberty of the masses in industry as well as in cultural goods. An era of power possessed by the few took the place of the era of liberty for all envisaged by the liberals of the early nineteenth century.

These statements do not imply that these liberals should or could have foreseen the changes that would occur, due to the impact of new forces of production. The point is that their failure to grasp the historic position of the interpretation of liberty they put forth served later to solidify a social régime that was a chief obstacle to attainment of the ends they professed. One aspect of this failure is worth especial mention. No one has ever seen more clearly than the Benthamites that the political self-interest of rulers, if not socially checked and controlled, leads to actions that destroy liberty for the mass of people. Their perception of this fact was a chief ground for their advocacy of representative government, for they saw in this measure a means by which the self-interest of the rulers would be forced into conformity with the interests of their subjects. But they had no glimpse of the fact that private control of the new forces of production, forces which affect the life of every one, would operate in the same way as private unchecked control of political power. They saw the need of new legal institutions, and of different political conditions as a means to political liberty. But they failed to perceive that social control of economic forces is equally necessary if anything approaching economic equality and liberty is to be realized.

Bentham did believe that increasing equalization of economic fortunes was desirable. He justified his opinion of its desirability on the ground of the greater happiness of the greater number: to put the matter crudely, the possession of ten thousand dollars by a thousand persons would generate a greater sum of happiness than the possession of ten million dollars by one person. But he believed that the régime of economic liberty would of itself tend in the direction of greater equalization. Meantime, he held that "time is the only mediator," and he opposed the use of organized social power to promote equalization on the ground that such action would disturb the "security" that is even a greater condition of happiness than is equality.

When it became evident that disparity, not equality, was the actual consequence of *laissez faire* liberalism, defenders of the latter developed a double system of justifying apologetics. Upon one front, they fell back upon the natural inequalities of individuals in psychological and moral make-up, asserting that inequality of fortune and economic status is the "natural" and justifiable consequence of the free play of these inherent differences. Herbert Spencer even erected this idea into a principle of cosmic justice, based upon the idea of the proportionate relation existing between cause and effect. I fancy that today there are but few who are hardy enough, even admitting the principle of natural inequalities, to assert that the disparities of property and income bear any commensurate ratio to inequalities in the native constitution of individuals. If we suppose that there is in fact such a ratio, the consequences are so intolerable that the practical inference to be drawn is that organized social effort should intervene to prevent the alleged natural law from taking full effect.

The other line of defense is unceasing glorification of the virtues of initiative, independence, choice and responsibility, virtues that centre in and proceed from individuals as such. I am one who believes that we need more, not fewer, "rugged individuals" and it is in the name of rugged individualism that I challenge the argument. Instead of independence, there exists parasitical dependence on a wide scale—witness the present need for the exercise of charity, private and public, on a vast scale. The current argument against the public dole on the ground that it pauperizes and demoralizes those who receive it has an ironical sound when it comes from those who would leave intact the conditions that cause the necessity for recourse to the method of support of millions at public expense. Servility and regimentation are the result of control by the few of access to means of productive labor on the part of the many. An even more serious objection to the argument is that it conceives of initiative, vigor, independence exclusively in terms of their least significant manifestation. They are limited to exercise in the economic area. The meaning of their exercise in connection with the cultural resources of civilization, in such matters as companionship, science and art, is all but ignored. It is at this last point in particular that the crisis of liberalism and the need for a reconsideration of it in terms of the genuine liberation of individuals are most evident. The enormous exaggeration of material and materialistic economics that now prevails at the expense of cultural values, is not itself the result of earlier liberalism. But, as was illustrated in the personal crisis through which Mill passed, it is an exaggeration which is favored, both intellectually and morally, by fixation of the early creed.

This fact induces a natural transition from the concept of liberty to that of the individual. The underlying philosophy and psychology of earlier liberalism led to a conception of individuality as something ready-made, already possessed, and needing only the removal of certain legal restrictions to come into full play. It was not conceived as a moving thing, something that is attained only by continuous growth. Because of this failure, the dependence in fact of individuals upon social conditions was made little of. It is true that some of the early liberals, like John Stuart Mill, made much of the effect of "circumstances" in producing differences among individuals. But the use of the word and idea of "circumstances" is significant. It suggests—and the context bears out the suggestion—that social arrangements and institutions were thought of as things that operate from without, not entering in any significant way into the internal make-up and growth of individuals. Social arrangements were treated not as positive forces but as external limitations. Some passages in Mill's discussion of the logic of the social sciences are pertinent. "Men in a state of society are still men; their actions and passions are obedient to the laws of individual human nature. Men are not, when brought together, converted into a different kind of substance, as hydrogen and oxygen differ from water. . . Human beings in society have no properties but those which are derived from, and may be resolved into, the laws of individual men." And again he says: "The actions and feelings of men in the social state are entirely governed by psychological laws."[1]

There is an implication in these passages that liberals will be the last to deny. This implication is directly in line with Mill's own revolt against the creed in which he was educated. As far as the statements are a warning against attaching undue importance to merely external institutional changes, to changes that do not enter into the desires, purposes and beliefs of the very constitution of individuals, they express an idea to which liberalism is committed by its own nature. But Mill means something at once less and more than this. While he would probably have

---

1. The quotations are from Mill's *Logic*, Book VI, chs. vii and ix.

denied that he held to the notion of a state of nature in which individuals exist prior to entering into a social state, he is in fact giving a psychological version of that doctrine. Individuals, it is implied, have a full-blown psychological and moral nature, having its own set laws, independently of their association with one another. It is the psychological laws of this isolated human nature from which social laws are derived and into which they may be resolved. His own illustration of water in its difference from hydrogen and oxygen on separation might have taught him better, if it had not been for the influence of a prior dogma. That the human infant is modified in mind and character by his connection with others in family life and that the modification continues throughout life as his connections with others broaden, is as true as that hydrogen is modified when it combines with oxygen. If we generalize the meaning of this fact, it is evident that while there are native organic or biological structures that remain fairly constant, the actual "laws" of human nature are laws of individuals in association, not of beings in a mythical condition apart from association. In other words, liberalism that takes its profession of the importance of individuality with sincerity must be deeply concerned about the structure of human association. For the latter operates to affect negatively and positively, the development of individuals. Because a wholly unjustified idea of opposition between individuals and society has become current, and because its currency has been furthered by the underlying philosophy of individualistic liberalism, there are many who in fact are working for social changes such that rugged individuals may exist in reality, that have become contemptuous of the very idea of individuality, while others support in the name of individualism institutions that militate powerfully against the emergence and growth of beings possessed of genuine individuality.

It remains to say something of the third enduring value in the liberal creed:—intelligence. Grateful recognition is due early liberals for their valiant battle in behalf of freedom of thought, conscience, expression and communication. The civil liberties we possess, however precariously today, are in large measure the fruit of their efforts and those of the French liberals who engaged in the same battle. But their basic theory as to the nature of intelligence is such as to offer no sure foundation for the permanent victory of the cause they espoused. They resolved mind into a complex of external associations among atomic elements, just as they resolved society itself into a similar compound of external associations among individuals, each of whom has his own independently fixed nature. Their psychology was not in fact the product of impartial inquiry into human nature. It was rather a political weapon devised in the interest of breaking down the rigidity of dogmas and of institutions that had lost their relevancy. Mill's own contention that psychological laws of the kind he laid down were prior to the laws of men living and communicating together, acting and reacting upon one another, was itself a political instrument forged in the interest of criticism of beliefs and institutions that he believed should be displaced. The doctrine was potent in exposure of abuses; it was weak for constructive purposes. Bentham's assertion that he introduced the method of experiment into the social sciences held good as far as resolution into atoms acting externally upon one another, after the Newtonian model, was concerned. It did not recognize the place in experiment of comprehensive social ideas as working hypotheses in direction of action.

The practical consequence was also the logical one. When conditions had changed and the problem was one of constructing social organization from individual units that had been released from old social ties, liberalism fell upon evil times. The conception of intelligence as something that arose from the association of isolated elements, sensations and feelings, left no room for far-reaching experiments in construction of a new social order. It was definitely hostile to everything like collective social planning. The doctrine of *laissez faire* was applied to intelligence as well as to economic action, although the conception of experimental method in science demands a control by comprehensive ideas, projected in possibilities to be realized by action. Scientific method is as much opposed to go-as-you-please in intellectual matters as it is to reliance upon habits of mind whose sanction is that they were formed by "experience" in the past. The theory of mind held by the early liberals advanced beyond dependence upon the past but it did not arrive at the idea of experimental and constructive intelligence.

The dissolving atomistic individualism of the liberal school evoked by way of reaction the theory of organic objective mind. But the effect of the latter theory embodied in idealistic metaphysics was also hostile to intentional social planning. The historical march of mind, embodied in institutions, was believed to account for social changes—all in its own good time. A similar conception was fortified by the interest in history and in evolution so characteristic of the later nineteenth century. The materialistic philosophy of Spencer joined hands with the idealistic doctrine of Hegel in throwing the burden of social direction upon powers that are beyond deliberate social foresight and planning. The economic dialectic of history, substituted by Marx for the Hegelian dialectic of ideas, as interpreted by the social-democratic party in Europe, was taken to signify an equally inevitable movement toward a predestined goal. Moreover, the idealistic theory of objective spirit provided an intellectual justification for the nationalisms that were rising. Concrete manifestation of absolute mind was said to be provided through national states. Today, this philosophy is readily turned to the support of the totalitarian state.

The crisis in liberalism is connected with failure to develop and lay hold of an adequate conception of intelligence integrated with social movements and a factor in giving them direction. We cannot mete out harsh blame to the early liberals for failure to attain such a conception. The first scientific society for the study of anthropology was founded the year in which Darwin's *Origin of Species* saw the light of day. I cite this particular fact to typify the larger fact that the sciences of society, the controlled study of man in his relationships, are the product of the later nineteenth century. Moreover, these disciplines not only came into being too late to influence the formulation of liberal social theory, but they themselves were so much under the influence of the more advanced physical sciences that it was supposed that their findings were of merely theoretic import. By this statement, I mean that although the conclusions of the social disciplines were about man, they were treated as if they were of the same nature as the conclusions of physical science about remote galaxies of stars. Social and historical inquiry is in fact a part of the social process itself, not something outside of it. The consequence of not perceiving this fact was that the conclusions of the social sciences were not made (and still are not made in any large measure) integral members of a program of social action. When the conclusions of inquiries that deal with man are left outside the program of social action, social policies are necessarily left without the guidance that knowledge of man can provide, and that it must provide if social action is not to be directed either by mere precedent and custom or else by the happy intuitions of individual minds. The social conception of the nature and work of intelligence is still miniature; in consequence, its use as a director of social action is inchoate and sporadic. It is the tragedy of earlier liberalism that just at the time when the problem of social organization was most urgent, liberals could bring to its solution nothing but the conception that intelligence is an individual possession.

It is all but a commonplace that today physical knowledge and its technical applications have far outrun our knowledge of man and its application in social invention and engineering. What I have just said indicates a deep source of the trouble. After all, our accumulated knowledge of man and his ways, furnished by anthropology, history, sociology and psychology, is vast, even though it be sparse in comparison with our knowledge of physical nature. But it is still treated as so much merely theoretic knowledge amassed by specialists, and at most communicated by them in books and articles to the general public. We are habituated to the idea that every discovery in physical knowledge signifies, sooner or later, a change in the processes of production; there are countless persons whose business it is to see that these discoveries take effect through invention in improved operations in practice. There is next to nothing of the same sort with respect to knowledge of man and human affairs. Although the latter is recognized to concern man in the sense of being *about* him, it is of less practical effect than are the much more remote findings of physical science.

The inchoate state of social knowledge is reflected in the

two fields where intelligence might be supposed to be most alert and most continuously active, education and the formation of social policies in legislation. Science is taught in our schools. But very largely it appears in schools simply as another study, to be acquired by much the same methods as are employed in "learning" the older studies that are part of the curriculum. If it were treated as what it is, the method of intelligence itself in action, then the method of science would be incarnate in every branch of study and every detail of learning. Thought would be connected with the possibility of action, and every mode of action would be reviewed to see its bearing upon the habits and ideas from which it sprang. Until science is treated educationally in this way, the introduction of what is called science into the schools signifies one more opportunity for the mechanization of the material and methods of study. When "learning" is treated not as an expansion of the understanding and judgment of meanings but as an acquisition of information, the method of cooperative experimental intelligence finds its way into the working structure of the individual only incidentally and by devious paths.

Of the place and use of socially organized intelligence in the conduct of public affairs, through legislation and administration, I shall have something to say in the next chapter. At this point of the discussion I am content to ask the reader to compare the force it now exerts in politics with that of the interest of individuals and parties in capturing and retaining office and power, with that exercised by the propaganda of publicity agents and that of organized pressure groups.

Humanly speaking, the crisis in liberalism was a product of particular historical events. Soon after liberal tenets were formulated as eternal truths, it became an instrument of vested interests in opposition to further social change, a ritual of lip-service, or else was shattered by new forces that came in. Nevertheless, the ideas of liberty, of individuality and of freed intelligence have an enduring value, a value never more needed than now. It is the business of liberalism to state these values in ways, intellectual and practical, that are relevant to present needs and forces. If we employ the conception of historic relativity, nothing is clearer than that the conception of liberty is always relative to forces that at a given time and place are increasingly felt to be oppressive. Liberty in the concrete signifies release from the impact of particular oppressive forces; emancipation from something once taken as a normal part of human life but now experienced as bondage. At one time, liberty signified liberation from chattel slavery; at another time, release of a class from serfdom. During the late seventeenth and early eighteenth centuries it meant liberation from despotic dynastic rule. A century later it meant release of industrialists from inherited legal customs that hampered the rise of new forces of production. Today, it signifies liberation from material insecurity and from the coercions and repressions that prevent multitudes from participation in the vast cultural resources that are at hand. The direct impact of liberty always has to do with some class or group that is suffering in a special way from some form of constraint exercised by the distribution of powers that exists in contemporary society. Should a classless society ever come into being the formal *concept* of liberty would lose its significance, because the *fact* for which it stands would have become an integral part of the established relations of human beings to one another.

Until such a time arrives liberalism will continue to have a necessary social office to perform. Its task is the mediation of social transitions. This phrase may seem to some to be a virtual admission that liberalism is a colorless "middle of the road" doctrine. Not so, even though liberalism has sometimes taken that form in practice. We are always dependent upon the experience that has accumulated in the past and yet there are always new forces coming in, new needs arising, that demand, if the new forces are to operate and the new needs to be satisfied, a reconstruction of the patterns of old experience. The old and the new have forever to be integrated with each other, so that the values of old experience may become the servants and instruments of new desires and aims. We are always possessed by habits and customs, and this fact signifies that we are always influenced by the inertia and the momentum of forces temporally outgrown but nevertheless still present with us as a part of our being. Human life gets set in patterns, institutional and moral. But change is also with us and demands the constant remaking of old habits and old ways of thinking, desiring and acting. The effective ratio between the old and the stabilizing and the new and disturbing is very different at different times. Sometimes whole communities seem to be dominated by custom, and changes are produced only by irruptions and invasions from outside. Sometimes, as at present, change is so varied and accelerated that customs seem to be dissolving before our very eyes. But be the ratio little or great, there is always an adjustment to be made, and as soon as the need for it becomes conscious, liberalism has a function and a meaning. It is not that liberalism creates the need, but that the necessity for adjustment defines the office of liberalism.

For the only adjustment that does not have to be made over again, and perhaps even under more unfavorable circumstances than when it was first attempted, is that effected through intelligence as a method. In its large sense, this remaking of the old through union with the new is precisely what intelligence is. It is conversion of past experience into knowledge and projection of that knowledge in ideas and purposes that anticipate what may come to be in the future and that indicate how to realize what is desired. Every problem that arises, personal or collective, simple or complex, is solved only by selecting material from the store of knowledge amassed in past experience and by bringing into play habits already formed. But the knowledge and the habits have to be modified to meet the new conditions that have arisen. In collective problems, the habits that are involved are traditions and institutions. The standing danger is either that they will be acted upon implicitly, without reconstruction to meet new conditions, or else that there will be an impatient and blind rush forward, directed only by some dogma rigidly adhered to. The office of intelligence in every problem that either a person or a community meets is to effect a working connection between old habits, customs, institutions, beliefs, and new conditions. What I have called the mediating function of liberalism is all one with the work of intelligence. This fact is the root, whether it be consciously realized or not, of the emphasis placed by liberalism upon the role of freed intelligence as the method of directing social action.

Objections that are brought against liberalism ignore the fact that the only alternatives to dependence upon intelligence are either drift and casual improvisation, or the use of coercive force stimulated by unintelligent emotion and fanatical dogmatism—the latter being intolerant by its very constitution. The objection that the method of intelligence has been tried and failed is wholly aside from the point, since the crux of the present situation is that it has not been tried under such conditions as now exist. It has not been tried at any time with use of all the resources that scientific material and the experimental method now put at our disposal. It is also said that intelligence is cold and that persons are moved to new ways of acting only by emotion, just as habit makes them adhere to old ways. Of course, intelligence does not generate action except as it is enkindled by feeling. But the notion that there is some inherent opposition between emotion and intelligence is a relic of the notion of mind that grew up before the experimental method of science had emerged. For the latter method signifies the union of ideas with action, a union that is intimate; and action generates and supports emotion. Ideas that are framed to be put into operation for the sake of guiding action are imbued with all the emotional force that attaches to the ends proposed for action, and are accompanied with all the excitement and inspiration that attends the struggle to realize the ends. Since the ends of liberalism are liberty and the opportunity of individuals to secure full realization of their potentialities, all of the emotional intensity that belongs to these ends gathers about the ideas and acts that are necessary to make them real.

Again, it is said that the average citizen is not endowed with the degree of intelligence that the use of it as a method demands. This objection, supported by alleged scientific findings about heredity and by impressive statistics concerning the intelligence quotient of the average citizen, rests wholly upon the old notion that intelligence is a ready-made possession of individuals. The last stand of oligarchical and anti-social seclusion is perpetuation of this purely individualistic notion of intelligence. The reliance of liberalism is not upon the mere abstraction of a native endowment unaffected by social relationships, but upon the fact that native capacity is sufficient to enable the average individual to respond to and to use the knowledge and the skill that are embodied in the social conditions in which he lives, moves and has his being. There are few individuals who have the native capacity that was required to invent the stationary steam-engine, locomotive, dynamo or telephone. But there are none so mean that they cannot intelligently utilize these embodiments of intelligence once they are a part of the organized means of associated living.

The indictments that are drawn against the intelligence of individuals are in truth indictments of a social order that does not permit the average individual to have access to the rich store of the accumulated wealth of mankind in knowledge, ideas and purposes. There does not now exist the kind of social organization that even permits the average human being to share the potentially available social intelligence. Still less is there a social order that has for one of its chief purposes the establishment of conditions that will move the mass of individuals to appropriate and use what is at hand. Back of the appropriation by the few of the material resources of society lies the appropriation by the few in behalf of their own ends of the cultural, the spiritual, resources that are the product not of the individuals who have taken possession but of the cooperative work of humanity. It is useless to talk about the failure of democracy until the source of its failure has been grasped and steps are taken to bring about that type of social organization that will encourage the socialized extension of intelligence.

The crisis in liberalism, as I said at the outset, proceeds from the fact that after early liberalism had done its work, society faced a new problem, that of social organization. Its work was to liberate a group of individuals, representing the new science and the new forces of productivity, from customs, ways of thinking, institutions, that were oppressive of the new modes of social action, however useful they may have been in their day. The instruments of analysis, of criticism, of dissolution, that were employed were effective for the work of release. But when it came to the problem of organizing the new forces and the individuals whose modes of life they radically altered into a coherent social organization, possessed of intellectual and moral directive power, liberalism was well-nigh impotent. The rise of national polities that pretend to represent the order, discipline and spiritual authority that will counteract social disintegration is a tragic comment upon the unpreparedness of older liberalism to deal with the new problem which its very success precipitated.

But the values of freed intelligence, of liberty, of opportunity for every individual to realize the potentialities of which he is possessed, are too precious to be sacrificed to a régime of despotism, especially when the régime is in such large measure merely the agent of a dominant economic class in its struggle to keep and extend the gains it has amassed' at the expense of genuine social order, unity, and development. Liberalism has to gather itself together to formulate the ends to which it is devoted in terms of means that are relevant to the contemporary situation. The only form of enduring social organization that is now possible is one in which the new forces of productivity are cooperatively controlled and used in the interest of the effective liberty and the cultural development of the individuals that constitute society. Such a social order cannot be established by an unplanned and external convergence of the actions of separate individuals, each of whom is bent on personal private advantage. This idea is the Achilles heel of early liberalism. The idea that liberalism cannot maintain its ends and at the same time reverse its conception of the means by which they are to be attained is folly. The ends can now be achieved *only* by reversal of the means to which early liberalism was committed. Organized social planning, put into effect for the creation of an order in which industry and finance are socially directed in behalf of institutions that provide the material basis for the cultural liberation and growth of individuals, is now the sole method of social action by which liberalism can realize its professed alms. Such planning demands in turn a new conception and logic of freed intelligence as a social force. To these phases of a renascent liberalism, I turn in the chapter that follows.

3.

Renascent Liberalism

Nothing is blinder than the supposition that we live in a society and world so static that either nothing new will happen or else it will happen because of the use of violence. Social change is here as a fact, a fact having multifarious forms and marked in intensity. Changes that are revolutionary in effect are in process in every phase of life. Transformations in the family, the church, the school, in science and art, in economic and political relations, are occurring so swiftly that imagination is baffled in attempt to lay hold of them. Flux does not have to be created. But it does have to be directed. It has to be so controlled that it will move to some end in accordance with the principles of life, since life itself is development. Liberalism is committed to an end that is at once enduring and flexible: the liberation of individuals so that realization of their capacities may be the law of their life. It is committed to the use of freed intelligence as the method of directing change. In any case, civilization is faced with the problem of uniting the changes that are going on into a coherent pattern of social organization.

The liberal spirit is marked by its own picture of the pattern that is required: a social organization that will make possible effective liberty and opportunity for personal growth in mind and spirit in all individuals. Its present need is recognition that established material security is a prerequisite of the ends which it cherishes, so that, the basis of life being secure, individuals may actively share in the wealth of cultural resources that now exist and may contribute, each in his own way, to their further enrichment.

The fact of change has been so continual and so intense that it overwhelms our minds. We are bewildered by the spectacle of its rapidity, scope and intensity. It is not surprising that men have protected themselves from the impact of such vast change by resorting to what psycho-analysis has taught us to call rationalizations, in other words, protective fantasies. The Victorian idea that change is a part of an evolution that necessarily leads through successive stages to some preordained divine far-off event is one rationalization. The conception of a sudden, complete, almost catastrophic, transformation, to be brought about by the victory of the proletariat over the class now dominant, is a similar rationalization. But men have met the impact of change in the realm of actuality, mostly by drift and by temporary, usually incoherent, improvisations. Liberalism, like every other theory of life, has suffered from the state of confused uncertainty that is the lot of a world suffering from rapid and varied change for which there is no intellectual and moral preparation.

Because of this lack of mental and moral preparation the impact of swiftly moving changes produced, as I have just said, confusion, uncertainty and drift. Change in patterns of belief, desire and purpose has lagged behind the modification of the external conditions under which men associate. Industrial habits have changed most rapidly; there has followed considerable distance, change in political relations; alterations in legal relations and methods have lagged even more, while changes in the institutions that deal most directly with patterns of thought and belief have taken place to the least extent. This fact defines the primary, though not by any means the ultimate, responsibility of a liberalism that intends to be a vital force. Its work is first of all education, in the broadest sense of that term. Schooling is a part of the work of education, but education in its full meaning includes all the influences that go to form the attitudes and dispositions (of desire as well as of belief), which constitute dominant habits of mind and character.

Let me mention three changes that have taken place in one of the institutions in which immense shifts have occurred, but that are still relatively external—external in the sense that the pattern of intelligent purpose and emotion has not been correspondingly modified. Civilization existed for most of human history in a state of scarcity in the material basis for a humane life. Our ways of thinking, planning and working have been attuned to this fact. Thanks to science and technology we now live in an age of potential plenty. The immediate effect of the emergence of the new possibility was simply to stimulate, to a point of incredible exaggeration, the striving for the material resources, called wealth, opened to men in the new vista. It is a characteristic of all development, physiological and mental, that when a new force and factor appears, it is first pushed to an extreme. Only when its possibilities have been exhausted (at least relatively) does it take its place in the life perspective. The economic-material phase of life, which belongs in the basal ganglia of society, has usurped for more than a century the cortex of the social body. The habits of desire and effort that were bred in the age of scarcity do not readily subordinate themselves and take the place of the matter-of-course routine that becomes appropriate to them when machines and impersonal power have the capacity to liberate man from bondage to the strivings that were once needed to make secure his physical basis. Even now when there is a vision of an age of abundance and when the vision is supported by hard fact, it is material security as an end that appeals to most rather than the way of living which this security makes possible. Men's minds are still pathetically held in the clutch of old habits and haunted by old memories.

For, in the second place, insecurity is the natural child and the foster child, too, of scarcity. Early liberalism emphasized the importance of insecurity as a fundamentally necessary economic motive, holding that without this goad men would not work, abstain or accumulate. Formulation of this conception was new. But the fact that was formulated was nothing new. It was deeply rooted in the habits that were formed in the long struggle against material scarcity. The system that goes by the name of capitalism is a systematic manifestation of desires and purposes built up in an age of ever threatening want and now carried over into a time of ever increasing potential plenty. The conditions that generate insecurity for the many no longer spring from nature. They are found in institutions and arrangements that are within deliberate human control. Surely this change marks one of the greatest revolutions that has taken place in all human history. Because of it, insecurity is not now the motive to work and sacrifice but to despair. It is not an instigation to put forth energy but to an impotency that can be converted from death into endurance only by charity. But the habits of mind and action that modify institutions to make potential abundance an actuality are still so inchoate that most of us discuss labels like individualism, socialism and communism instead of even perceiving the possibility, much less the necessity for realizing what can and should be.

In the third place, the patterns of belief and purpose that still dominate economic institutions were formed when individuals produced with their hands, alone or in small groups. The notion that society in general is served by the unplanned coincidence of the consequences of a vast multitude of efforts put forth by isolated individuals without reference to any social end, was also something new as a formulation. But it also formulated the working principle of an epoch which the advent of new forces of production was to bring to an end. It demands no great power of intelligence to see that under present conditions the isolated individual is well-nigh helpless. Concentration and corporate organization are the rule. But the concentration and corporate organization are still controlled in their operation by ideas that were institutionalized in eons of separate individual effort. The attempts at cooperation for mutual benefit that are put forth are precious as experimental moves. But that society itself should see to it that a cooperative industrial order be instituted, one that is consonant with the realities of production enforced by an era of machinery and power, is so novel an idea to the general mind that its mere suggestion is hailed with abusive epithets—sometimes with imprisonment.

When, then, I say that the first object of a renascent liberalism is education, I mean that its task is to aid in producing the habits of mind and character, the intellectual and moral patterns, that are somewhere near even with the actual move-

ments of events. It is, I repeat, the split between the latter as
they have externally occurred and the ways of desiring, thinking, and of putting emotion and purpose into execution that is
the basic cause of present confusion in mind and paralysis in
action. The educational task cannot be accomplished merely
by working upon men's minds, without action that effects
actual change in institutions. The idea that dispositions and
attitudes can be altered by merely "moral" means conceived of
as something that goes on wholly inside of persons is itself one
of the old patterns that has to be changed. Thought, desire and
purpose exist in a constant give and take of interaction with
environing conditions. But resolute thought is the first step in
that change of action that will itself carry further the needed
change in patterns of mind and character.

In short, liberalism must now become radical, meaning by
"radical" perception of the necessity of thoroughgoing changes
in the set-up of institutions and corresponding activity to bring
the changes to pass. For the gulf between what the actual situation makes possible and the actual state itself is so great that
it cannot be bridged by piecemeal policies undertaken *ad hoc*.
The process of producing the changes will be, in any case, a
gradual one. But "reforms" that deal now with this abuse and
now with that without having a social goal based upon an
inclusive plan, differ entirely from effort at re-forming, in its lit-
eral sense, the institutional scheme of things. The liberals of
more than a century ago were denounced in their time as sub-
versive radicals, and only when the new economic order was
established did they become apologists for the *status quo* or
else content with social patchwork. If radicalism be defined as
perception of need for radical change, then today any liberalism which is not also radicalism is irrelevant and doomed.

But radicalism also means, in the minds of many, both sup-
porters and opponents, dependence upon use of violence as the
main method of effecting drastic changes. Here the liberal
parts company. For he is committed to the organization of
intelligent action as the chief method. Any frank discussion of
the issue must recognize the extent to which those who decry
the use of any violence are themselves willing to resort to violence and are ready to put their will into operation. Their fundamental objection is to change in the economic institution
that now exists, and for its maintenance they resort to the use
of the force that is placed in their hands by this very institution.
They do not need to advocate the use of force; their only need
is to employ it. Force, rather than intelligence, is built into the
procedures of the existing social system, regularly as coercion,
in times of crisis as overt violence. The legal system, conspic-
uously in its penal aspect, more subtly in civil practice, rests
upon coercion. Wars are the methods recurrently used in set-
tlement of disputes between nations. One school of radicals
dwells upon the fact that in the past the transfer of power in
one society has either been accomplished by or attended with
violence. But what we need to realize is that physical force is
used, at least in the form of coercion, in the very set-up of our
society. That the competitive system, which was thought of by
early liberals as the means by which the latent abilities of individuals were to be evoked and directed into socially useful
channels, is now in fact a state of scarcely disguised battle
hardly needs to be dwelt upon. That the control of the means
of production by the few in legal possession operates as a standing agency of coercion of the many, may need emphasis in
statement, but is surely evident to one who is willing to observe
and honestly report the existing scene. It is foolish to regard the

political state as the only agency now endowed with coercive power. Its exercise of this power is pale in contrast with that exercised by concentrated and organized property interests.

It is not surprising in view of our standing dependence upon the use of coercive force that at every time of crisis coercion breaks out into open violence. In this country, with its tradition of violence fostered by frontier conditions and by the conditions under which immigration went on during the greater part of our history, resort to violence is especially recurrent on the part of those who are in power. In times of imminent change, our verbal and sentimental worship of the Constitution, with its guarantees of civil liberties of expression, publication and assemblage, readily goes overboard. Often the officials of the law are the worst offenders, acting as agents of some power that rules the economic life of a community. What is said about the value of free speech as a safety valve is then forgotten with the utmost of ease: a comment, perhaps, upon the weakness of the defense of freedom of expression that values it simply as a means of blowing-off steam.

It is not pleasant to face the extent to which, as matter of fact, coercive and violent force is relied upon in the present social system as a means of social control. It is much more agreeable to evade the fact. But unless the fact is acknowledged as a fact in its full depth and breadth, the meaning of dependence upon intelligence as the alternative method of social direction will not be grasped. Failure in acknowledgment signifies, among other things, failure to realize that those who propagate the dogma of dependence upon force have the sanction of much that is already entrenched in the existing system. They would but turn the use of it to opposite ends. The assumption that the method of intelligence already rules and that those who urge the use of violence are introducing a new element into the social picture may not be hypocritical but it is unintelligently unaware of what is actually involved in intelligence as an alternative method of social action.

I begin with an example of what is really involved in the issue. Why is it, apart from our tradition of violence, that liberty of expression is tolerated and even lauded when social affairs seem to be going in a quiet fashion, and yet is so readily destroyed whenever matters grow critical? The general answer, of course, is that at bottom social institutions have habituated us to the use of force in some veiled form. But a part of the answer is found in our ingrained habit of regarding intelligence as an individual possession and its exercise as an individual right. It is false that freedom of inquiry and of expression are not modes of action. They are exceedingly potent modes of action. The reactionary grasps this fact, in practice if not in express idea, more quickly than the liberal, who is too much given to holding that this freedom is innocent of consequences, as well as being a merely individual right. The result is that this liberty is tolerated as long as it does not seem to menace in any way the *status quo* of society. When it does, every effort is put forth to identify the established order with the public good. When this identification is established, it follows that any merely individual right must yield to the general welfare. As long as freedom of thought and speech is claimed as a merely individual right, it will give way, as do other merely personal claims, when it is, or is successfully represented to be, in opposition to the general welfare.

I would not in the least disparage the noble fight waged by early liberals in behalf of individual freedom of thought and expression. We owe more to them than it is possible to record in words. No more eloquent words have ever come from any one than those of Justice Brandeis in the case of a legislative act that in fact restrained freedom of political expression. He said: "Those who won our independence believed that the final end of the State was to make men free to develop their faculties, and that in its government the deliberative forces should prevail over the arbitrary. They valued liberty both as an end and as a means. They believed liberty to be the secret of happiness and courage to be the secret of liberty. They believed that freedom to think as you will and to speak as you think are means indispensable to the discovery and spread of political truth; that without free speech and assembly discussion would be futile; that with them, discussion affords ordinarily adequate protection against the dissemination of noxious doctrines; that the greatest menace to freedom is ail inert people; that public discussion is a political duty; and that this should be a fundamental principle of the American Government." This is the creed of a fighting liberalism. But the issue I am raising is connected with the fact that these words are found in a dissenting, a minority opinion of the Supreme Court of the United States. The public function of free individual thought and speech is clearly recognized in the words quoted. But the reception of the truth of the words is met by an obstacle: the old habit of defending liberty of thought and expression as something inhering in individuals apart from and even in opposition to social claims.

Liberalism has to assume the responsibility for making it clear that intelligence is a social asset and is clothed with a function as public as is its origin, in the concrete, in social cooperation. It was Comte who, in reaction against the purely individualistic ideas that seemed to him to underlie the French

Revolution, said that in mathematics, physics and astronomy there is no right of private conscience. If we remove the statement from the context of actual scientific procedure, it is dangerous because it is false. The individual inquirer has not only the right but the duty to criticize the ideas, theories and "laws" that are current in science. But if we take the statement in the context of scientific method, it indicates that he carries on this criticism in virtue of a socially generated body of knowledge and by means of methods that are not of private origin and possession. He uses a method that retains public validity even when innovations are introduced in its use and application.

Henry George, speaking of ships that ply the ocean with a velocity of five or six hundred miles a day, remarked, "There is nothing whatever to show that the men who to-day build and navigate and use such ships are one whit superior in any physical or mental quality to their ancestors, whose best vessel was a coracle of wicker and hide. The enormous improvement which these ships show is not an improvement of human nature; it is an improvement of society—it is due to a wider and fuller union of individual efforts in accomplishment of common ends." This single instance, duly pondered, gives a better idea of the nature of intelligence and its social office than would a volume of abstract dissertation. Consider merely two of the factors that enter in and their social consequences. Consider what is involved in the production of steel, from the first use of fire and then the crude smelting of ore, to the processes that now effect the mass production of steel. Consider also the development of the power of guiding ships across trackless wastes from the day when they hugged the shore, steering by visible sun and stars, to the appliances that now enable a sure course to be taken. It would require a heavy tome to describe the advances in science, in mathematics, astronomy, physics, chemistry, that have made these two things possible. The record would be an account of a vast multitude of cooperative efforts, in which one individual uses the results provided for him by a countless number of other individuals, and uses them so as to add to the common and public store. A survey of such facts brings home the actual social character of intelligence as it actually develops and makes its way. Survey of the consequences upon the ways of living of individuals and upon the terms on which men associate together, due to the new method of transportation would take us to the wheat farmer of the prairies, the cattle raiser of the plains, the cotton grower of the South; into a multitude of mills and factories, and to the counting-room of banks, and what would be seen in this country would be repeated in every country of the globe.

It is to such things as these, rather than to abstract and formal psychology that we must go if we would learn the nature of intelligence: in itself, in its origin and development, and its uses and consequences. At this point, I should like to recur to an idea put forward in the preceding chapter. I then referred to the contempt often expressed for reliance upon intelligence as a social method, and I said this scorn is due to the identification of intelligence with native endowments of individuals. In contrast to this notion, I spoke of the power of individuals to appropriate and respond to the intelligence, the knowledge, ideas and purposes that have been integrated in the medium in which individuals live.

Each of us knows, for example, some mechanic of ordinary native capacity who is intelligent within the matters of his calling. He has lived in an environment in which the cumulative intelligence of a multitude of cooperating individuals is embodied, and by the use of his native capacities he makes some phase of this intelligence his own. Given a social medium in whose institutions the available knowledge, ideas and art of humanity were incarnate, and the average individual would rise to undreamed heights of social and political intelligence.

The rub, the problem is found in the proviso. Can the intelligence actually existent and potentially available be embodied in that institutional medium in which an individual thinks, desires and acts? Before dealing directly with this question, I wish to say something about the operation of intelligence in our present political institutions, as exemplified by current practices of democratic government. I would not minimize the advance scored in substitution of methods of discussion and conference for the method of arbitrary rule. But the better is too often the enemy of the still better. Discussion, as the manifestation of intelligence in political life, stimulates publicity; by its means sore spots are brought to light that would otherwise remain hidden. It affords opportunity for promulgation of new ideas. Compared with despotic rule, it is an invitation to individuals to concern themselves with public affairs. But discussion and dialectic, however indispensable they are to the elaboration of ideas and policies after ideas are once put forth, are weak reeds to depend upon for systematic origination of comprehensive plans, the plans that are required if the problem of social organization is to be met. There was a time when discussion, the comparison of ideas already current so is to purify and clarify them, was thought to be sufficient in discovery of the structure and laws of physical nature. In the latter field, the method was displaced by that of experimental observation guided by comprehensive working hypotheses, and using all the resources made available by mathematics.

But we still depend upon the method of discussion, with only incidental scientific control, in politics. Our system of popular suffrage, immensely valuable as it is in comparison with what preceded it, exhibits the idea that intelligence is an individualistic possession, at best enlarged by public discussion. Existing political practice, with its complete ignoring of occupational groups and the organized knowledge and purposes that are involved in the existence of such groups, manifests a dependence upon a summation of individuals quantitatively, similar to Bentham's purely quantitative formula of the greatest sum of pleasures of the greatest possible number. The formation of parties or, as the eighteenth-century writers called them, factions, and the system of party government is the practically necessary counterweight to a numerical and atomistic individualism. The idea that the conflict of parties will, by means of public discussion, bring out necessary public truths is a kind of political watered-down version of the Hegelian dialectic, with its synthesis arrived at by a union of antithetical conceptions. The method has nothing in common with the procedure of organized cooperative inquiry which has won the triumphs of science in the field of physical nature. Intelligence in politics when it is identified with discussion means reliance upon symbols. The invention of language is probably the greatest single invention achieved by humanity. The development of political forms that promote the use of symbols in place of arbitrary power was another great invention. The nineteenth-century establishment of parliamentary institutions, written constitutions and the suffrage as means of political rule, is a tribute to the power of symbols. But symbols are significant only in connection with realities behind them. No intelligent observer can deny, I think, that they are often used in party politics as a substitute for realities instead of as means of contact with them. Popular literacy, in connection with the telegraph, cheap postage and the printing press, has enormously multiplied the number of those influenced. That which we term education has done a good deal to generate habits that put symbols in the place of realities. The forms of popular government make necessary the elaborate use of words to influence political action. "Propaganda" is the inevitable consequence of the combination of these influences and it extends to every area of life. Words not only take the place of realities but are themselves debauched. Decline in the prestige of suffrage and of parliamentary government are intimately associated with the belief, manifest in practice even if not expressed in words, that intelligence is an individual possession to be reached by means of verbal persuasion.

This fact suggests, by way of contrast, the genuine meaning of intelligence in connection with public opinion, sentiment and action. The crisis in democracy demands the substitution of the intelligence that is exemplified in scientific procedure for the kind of intelligence that is now accepted. The need for this change is not exhausted in the demand for greater honesty and impartiality, even though these qualities be now corrupted by discussion carried on mainly for purposes of party supremacy and for imposition of some special but concealed interest. These qualities need to be restored. But the need goes further. The social use of intelligence would remain deficient even if these moral traits were exalted, and yet intelligence continued to be identified simply with discussion and persuasion, necessary as are these things. Approximation to use of scientific method in investigation and of the engineering mind in the invention and projection of far-reaching social plans is demanded. The habit of considering social realities in terms of cause and effect and social policies in terms of means and consequences is still inchoate. The contrast between the state of intelligence in politics and in the physical control of nature is to be taken literally. What has happened in this latter is the outstanding demonstration of the meaning of organized intelligence. The combined effect of science and technology has released more productive energies in a bare hundred years than stands to the credit of prior human history in its entirety. Productively it has multiplied nine million times in the last generation alone. The prophetic vision of Francis Bacon of subjugation of the energies of nature through change in methods of inquiry has well-nigh been realized. The stationary engine, the locomotive, the dynamo, the motor car, turbine, telegraph, telephone, radio and moving picture are not the products of either isolated individual minds nor of the particular economic regime called capitalism. They are the fruit of methods that first penetrated to the working causalities of nature and then utilized the resulting knowledge in bold imaginative ventures of invention and construction.

We hear a great deal in these days about class conflict. The past history of man is held up to us as almost exclusively a record of struggles between classes, ending in the victory of a class that had been oppressed and the transfer of power to it. It is difficult to avoid reading the past in terms of the contemporary scene. Indeed, fundamentally it is impossible to avoid this course. With a certain proviso, it is highly important that we are compelled to follow this path. For the past as past is gone, save for esthetic enjoyment and refreshment, while the present is with us. Knowledge of the past is significant only as it deepens and extends our understanding of the present. Yet there is a proviso. We must grasp the things that are most important in the present when we turn to the past and not allow ourselves to be misled by secondary phenomena no matter how intense and immediately urgent they are. Viewed from this standpoint, the rise of scientific method and of technology based upon it is the genuinely active force in producing the vast complex of changes the world is now undergoing, not the class struggle whose spirit and method are opposed to science. If we lay hold upon the causal force exercised by this embodiment of intelligence we shall know where to turn for the means of directing further change.

When I say that scientific method and technology have been the active force in producing the revolutionary transformations society is undergoing, I do not imply no other forces have been at work to arrest, deflect and corrupt their operation. Rather this fact is positively implied. At this point, indeed, is located the conflict that underlies the confusions and uncertainties of the present scene. The conflict is between institutions and habits originating in the pre-scientific and pre-technological age and the new forces generated by science and technology. The application of science, to a considerable degree, even its own growth, has been conditioned by the system to which the name of capitalism is given, a rough designation of a complex of political and legal arrangements centering about a particular mode of economic relations. Because of the conditioning of science and technology by this setting, the second and humanly most important part of Bacon's prediction has so far largely missed realization. The conquest of natural energies has not accrued to the betterment of the common human estate in anything like the degree he anticipated.

Because of conditions that were set by the legal institutions and the moral ideas existing when the scientific and industrial revolutions came into being, the chief usufruct of the latter has

been appropriated by a relatively small class. Industrial entre-
preneurs have reaped out of all proportion to what they sowed.
By obtaining private ownership of the means of production
and exchange they deflected a considerable share of the results
of increased productivity to their private pockets. This appropriation was not the fruit of criminal conspiracy or of sinister
intent. It was sanctioned not only by legal institutions of age-
long standing but by the entire prevailing, moral code. The
institution of private property long antedated feudal times. It is
the institution with which men have lived, with few excep-
tions, since the dawn of civilization. Its existence has deeply
impressed itself upon mankind's moral conceptions. Moreover,
the new industrial forces tended to break down many of the
rigid class barriers that had been in force, and to give to millions
a new outlook and inspire a new hope;—especially in this country with no feudal background and no fixed class system.

   Since the legal institutions and the patterns of mind characteristic of ages of civilization still endure, there exists the
conflict that brings confusion into every phase of present life.
The problem of bringing into being a new social orientation
and organization is, when reduced to its ultimates, the problem
of using the new resources of production, made possible by the
advance of physical science, for social ends, for what Bentham
called the greatest good of the greatest number. Institutional
relationships fixed in the pre-scientific age stand in the way of
accomplishing this great transformation. Lag in mental and
moral patterns provides the bulwark of the older institutions;
in expressing the past they still express present beliefs, outlooks
and purposes. Here is the place where the problem of liberalism centers today.

   The argument drawn from past history that radical change

must be effected by means of class struggle, culminating in open war, fails to discriminate between the two forces, one active, the other resistant and deflecting, that have produced the social scene in which we live. The active force is, as I have said, scientific method and technological application. The opposite force is that of older institutions and the habits that have grown up around them. Instead of discrimination between forces and distribution of their consequences, we find the two things lumped together. The compound is labeled the capitalistic or the bourgeois class, and to this class as a class is imputed all the important features of present industrialized society— much as the defenders of the régime of economic liberty exercised for private property are accustomed to attribute every improvement made in the last century and a half to the same capitalistic régime. Thus in orthodox communist literature, from the *Communist Manifesto* of 1848 to the present day, we are told that the bourgeoisie, the name for a distinctive class, has done this and that. It has, so it is said, given a cosmopolitan character to production and consumption; has destroyed the national basis of industry; has agglomerated population in urban centers; has transferred power from the country to the city, in the process of creating colossal productive force, its chief achievement. In addition, it has created crises of ever renewed intensity; has created imperialism of a new type in frantic effort to control raw materials and markets. Finally, it has created a new class, the proletariat, and has created it as a class having a common interest opposed to that of the bourgeoisie, and is giving an irresistible stimulus to its organization, first as a class and then as a political power. According to the economic version of the Hegelian dialectic, the bourgeois class is thus creating its own complete and polar opposite, and this in time will end the old power and rule. The class struggle of veiled civil war will finally burst into open revolution and the result will be either the common ruin of the contending parties or a revolutionary reconstitution of society at large through a transfer of power from one class to another.

The position thus sketched unites vast sweep with great simplicity. I am concerned with it here only as far as it emphasizes the idea of a struggle between classes, culminating in open and violent warfare as being the method for production of radical social change. For, be it noted, the issue is not whether some amount of violence will accompany the effectuation of radical change of institutions. The question is whether force or intelligence is to be the method upon which we consistently rely and to whose promotion we devote our energies. Insistence that the use of violent force is *inevitable* limits the use of available intelligence, for wherever the inevitable reigns intelligence cannot be used. Commitment to inevitability is always the fruit of dogma; intelligence does not pretend to *know* save as a result of experimentation, the opposite of preconceived dogma. Moreover, acceptance in advance of the inevitability of violence tends to produce the use of violence in cases where peaceful methods might otherwise avail. The curious fact is that while it is generally admitted that this and that particular social problem, say of the family, or railroads or banking, must be solved, if at all, by the method of intelligence, yet there is supposed to be some one all-inclusive social problem which can be solved only by the use of violence. This fact would be inexplicable were it not a conclusion from dogma as its premise.

It is frequently asserted that the method of experimental intelligence can be applied to physical facts because physical nature does not present conflicts of class interests, while it is inapplicable to society because the latter is so deeply marked by incompatible interests. It is then assumed that the "experimentalist" is one who has chosen to ignore the uncomfortable fact of conflicting interests. Of course, there *are* conflicting interests; otherwise there would be no social problems. The problem under discussion is precisely *how* conflicting claims are to be settled in the interest of the widest possible contribution to the interests of all—or at least of the great majority. The method of democracy—inasfar as it is that of organized intelligence—is to bring these conflicts out into the open where their special claims can be seen and appraised, where they can be discussed and judged in the light of more inclusive interests than are represented by either of them separately. There is, for example, a clash of interests between munition manufacturers and most of the rest of the population. The more the respective claims of the two are publicly and scientifically weighed, the more likely it is that the public interest will be disclosed and be made effective. There is an undoubted objective clash of interests between finance-capitalism that controls the means of production and whose profit is served by maintaining relative scarcity, and idle workers and hungry consumers. But what generates violent strife is failure to bring the conflict into the light of intelligence where the conflicting interests can be adjudicated in behalf of the interest of the great majority. Those most committed to the dogma of inevitable force recognize the need for intelligently discovering and expressing the dominant social interest up to a certain point and then draw back. The "experimentalist" is one who would see to it that the method depended upon by all in some degree in every democratic community be followed through to completion.

In spite of the existence of class conflicts, amounting at

times to veiled civil war, any one habituated to the use of the method of science will view with considerable suspicion the erection of actual human beings into fixed entities called classes, having no overlapping interests and so internally unified and externally separated that they are made the protagonists of history—itself hypothetical. Such an idea of classes is a survival of a rigid logic that once prevailed in the sciences of nature, but that no longer has any place there. This conversion of abstractions into entities smells more of a dialectic of concepts than of a realistic examination of facts, even though it makes more of an emotional appeal to many than do the results of the latter. To say that all past historic social progress has been the result of cooperation and not of conflict would be also an exaggeration. But exaggeration against exaggeration, it is the more reasonable of the two. And it is no exaggeration to say that the measure of civilization is the degree in which the method of cooperative intelligence replaces the method of brute conflict.

But the point I am especially concerned with just here is the indiscriminate lumping together as a single force of two different things—the results of scientific technology and of a legal system of property relations. It is science and technology that have had the revolutionary social effect while the legal system has been the relatively static element. According to the Marxians themselves, the economic foundations of society consist of two things, the forces of production on one side and, on the other side, the social relations of production, that is, the legal property system under which the former operates. The latter tags behind, and "revolutions" are produced by the power of the forces of production to change the system of institutional relations. But what are the modern forces of production save those of scientific technology? And what is scientific technology save a large-scale demonstration of organized intelligence in action?

It is quite true that what is happening socially is the result of the combination of the two factors, one dynamic, the other relatively static. If we choose to call the combination by the name of capitalism, then it is true, or a truism, that capitalism is the "cause" of all the important social changes that have occurred—an argument that the representatives of capitalism are eager to put forward whenever the increase of productivity is in question. But if we want to *understand*, and not just to paste labels, unfavorable or favorable as the case may be, we shall certainly begin and end with discrimination. Colossal increase in productivity, the bringing of men together in cities and large factories, the elimination of distance, the accumulation of capital, fixed and liquid—these things would have come about, at a certain stage, no matter what the established institutional system. They are the consequence of the new means of technological production. Certain other things have happened because of institutions and the habits of belief and character that accompany and support them. If we begin at this point, we shall see that the release of productivity is the product of cooperatively organized intelligence, and shall also see that the institutional framework is precisely that which is not subjected as yet, in any considerable measure, to the impact of inventive and constructive intelligence. That coercion and oppression on a large scale exist, no honest person can deny. But these things are not the product of science and technology but of the perpetuation of old institutions and patterns untouched by scientific method. The inference to be drawn is clear.

The argument, drawn from history, that great social changes have been effected only by violent means, needs considerable qualification, in view of the vast scope of changes that are taking place without the use of violence. But even if it be admitted to hold of the past, the conclusion that violence is the method now to be depended upon does not follow—unless one is committed to a dogmatic philosophy of history. The radical who insists that the future method of change must be like that of the past has much in common with the hide-bound reactionary who holds to the past as an ultimate fact. Both overlook the *fact that history in being a process of change generates change not only in details but also in the method of directing social change.* I recur to what I said at the beginning of this chapter. It is true that the social order is largely conditioned by the use of coercive force, bursting at times into open violence. But what is also true is that mankind now has in its possession a new method, that of cooperative and experimental science which expresses the method of intelligence. I should be meeting dogmatism with dogmatism if I asserted that the existence of this historically new factor completely invalidates all arguments drawn from the effect of force in the past. But it is within the bounds of reason to assert that the presence of this social factor demands that the present situation be analyzed on its own terms, and not be rigidly subsumed under fixed conceptions drawn from the past.

Any analysis made in terms of the present situation will not fail to note one fact that militates powerfully against arguments drawn from past use of violence. Modern warfare is destructive beyond anything known in older times. This increased destructiveness is due primarily, of course, to the fact that science has raised to a new pitch of destructive power all the agencies of armed hostility. But it also due to the much greater interdependence of all the elements of society. The bonds that hold modern communities and states together are as delicate as they are numerous. The self-sufficiency and independence of a local community, characteristic of more primitive societies, have disappeared in every highly industrialized country. The gulf that once separated the civilian population from the military has virtually gone. War involves paralysis of all normal social activities, and not merely the meeting of armed forces in the field. The *Communist Manifesto* presented two alternatives: *either* the revolutionary change and transfer of power to the proletariat, *or* the common ruin of the contending parties. Today, the civil war that would be adequate to effect transfer of power and a reconstitution of society at large, as understood by official Communists, would seem to present but one possible consequence: the ruin of all parties and the destruction of civilized life. This fact alone is enough to lead us to consider the potentialities of the method of intelligence.

The argument for putting chief dependence upon violence as the method of effecting radical change is, moreover, usually put in a way that proves altogether too much for its own case. It is said that the dominant economic class has all the agencies of power in its hands, directly the army, militia and police; indirectly, the courts, schools, press and radio. I shall not stop to analyze this statement. But if one admits it to be valid, the conclusion to be drawn is surely the folly of resorting to a use of force against force that is so well intrenched. The positive conclusion that emerges is that conditions that would promise success in the case of use of force are such as to make possible great change without any great recourse to such a method.[1]

---

1. It should be noted that Marx himself was not completely committed to the dogma of the inevitability of force as the means of effecting revolutionary changes in the system of "social relations." For at one time he contemplated that the change might occur in Great Britain and the United States, and possibly in Holland, by peaceful means.

Those who uphold the necessity of dependence upon violence usually much oversimplify the case by setting up a disjunction they regard as self-evident. They say that the sole alternative is putting our trust in parliamentary procedures as they now exist. This isolation of law-making from other social forces and agencies that are constantly operative is wholly unrealistic. Legislatures and congresses do not exist in a vacuum—not even the judges on the bench live in completely secluded sound-proof chambers. The assumption that it is possible for the constitution and activities of law-making bodies to persist unchanged while society itself is undergoing great change is an exercise in verbal formal logic.

It is true that in this country, because of the interpretations made by courts of a written constitution, our political institutions are unusually inflexible. It Is also true, as well as even more important (because it is a factor in causing this rigidity) that our institutions, democratic in form, tend to favor in substance a privileged plutocracy. Nevertheless, it is sheer defeatism to assume in advance of actual trial that democratic political institutions are incapable either of further development or of constructive social application. Even as they now exist, the forms of representative government are potentially capable of expressing the public will when that assumes anything like unification. And there is nothing inherent in them that forbids their supplementation by political agencies that represent definitely economic social interests, like those of producers and consumers.

The final argument in behalf of the use of intelligence is that as are the means used so are the actual ends achieved—that is, the consequences. I know of no greater fallacy than the claim of those who hold to the dogma of the necessity of brute force that this use will be the method of calling genuine democracy into existence—of which they profess themselves the simon-pure adherents. It requires an unusually credulous faith in the Hegelian dialectic of opposites to think that all of a sudden the use of force by a class will be transmuted into a democratic classless society. Force breeds counterforce; the Newtonian law of action and reaction still holds in physics, and violence is physical. To profess democracy as an ultimate ideal and the suppression of democracy as a means to the ideal may be possible in a country that has never known even rudimentary democracy, but when professed in a country that has anything of a genuine democratic spirit in its traditions, it signifies desire for possession and retention of power by a class, whether that class be called Fascist or Proletarian. In the light of what happens in non-democratic countries, it is pertinent to ask whether the rule of a class signifies the dictatorship of the majority, or dictatorship over the chosen class by a minority party; whether dissenters are allowed even within the class the party claims to represent; and whether the development of literature and the other arts proceeds according to a formula prescribed by a party in conformity with a doctrinaire dogma of history and of infallible leadership, or whether artists are free from regimentation? Until these questions are satisfactorily answered, it is permissible to look with considerable suspicion upon those who assert that suppression of democracy is the road to the adequate establishment of genuine democracy. The one exception—and that apparent rather than real—to dependence upon organized intelligence as the method for directing social change is found when society through an authorized majority has entered upon the path of social experimentation leading to great social change, and a minority refuses by force to permit the method of intelligent action to go into effect. Then force may be intelligently employed to subdue and disarm the recalcitrant minority.

There may be some who think I am unduly dignifying a position held by a comparatively small group by taking their arguments as seriously as I have done. But their position serves to bring into strong relief the alternatives before us. It makes clear the meaning of renascent liberalism. The alternatives are continuation of drift with attendant improvisations to meet special emergencies; dependence upon violence; dependence upon socially organized intelligence. The first two alternatives, however, are not mutually exclusive, for if things are allowed to drift the result may be some sort of social change effected by the use of force, whether so planned or not. Upon the whole, the recent policy of liberalism has been to further "social legislation"; that is, measures which add performance of social services to the older functions of government. The value of this addition is not to be despised. It marks a decided move away from *laissez faire* liberalism, and has considerable importance in educating the public mind to a realization of the possibilities of organized social control. It has helped to develop some of the techniques that in any case will be needed in a socialized economy. But the cause of liberalism will be lost for a considerable period if it is not prepared to go further and socialize the forces of production, now at hand, so that the liberty of individuals will be supported by the very structure of economic organization.

The ultimate place of economic organization in human life is to assure the secure basis for an ordered expression of individual capacity and for the satisfaction of the needs of man in noneconomic directions. The effort of mankind in connection with material production belongs, as I said earlier, among interests and activities that are, relatively speaking, routine in character, "routine" being defined as that which, without absorbing attention and energy, provides a constant basis for liberation of the values of intellectual, esthetic and companionship life. Every significant religious and moral teacher and prophet has asserted that the material is instrumental to the good life. Nominally at least, this idea is accepted by every civilized community. The transfer of the burden of material production from human muscles and brain to steam, electricity and chemical processes now makes possible the effective actualization of this ideal. Needs, wants and desires are always the moving force in generating creative action. When these wants are compelled by force of conditions to be directed for the most part, among the mass of mankind, into obtaining the means of subsistence, what should be a means becomes perforce an end in itself. Up to the present the new mechanical forces of production, which are the means of emancipation from this state of affairs, have been employed to intensify and exaggerate the reversal of the true relation between means and ends. Humanly speaking, I do not see how it would have been possible to avoid an epoch having this character. But its perpetuation is the cause of the continually growing social chaos and strife. Its termination cannot be effected by preaching to individuals that they should place spiritual ends above material means. It can be brought about by organized social reconstruction that puts the results of the mechanism of abundance at the free disposal of individuals. The actual corrosive "materialism" of our times does not proceed from science. It springs from the notion, sedulously cultivated by the class in power, that the creative capacities of individuals can be evoked and developed only in a struggle for material possessions and material gain. We either should surrender our professed belief in the supremacy of ideal and spiritual values and accommodate our beliefs to the predominant material orientation, or we should through organized endeavor institute the socialized economy of material security and plenty that will release human energy for pursuit of higher values.

Since liberation of the capacities of individuals for free, self-initiated expression is an essential part of the creed of liberalism, liberalism that is sincere must will the means that condition the achieving of its ends. Regimentation of material and mechanical forces is the only way by which the mass of individuals can be released from regimentation and consequent suppression of their cultural possibilities. The eclipse of liberalism is due to the fact that it has not faced the alternatives and adopted the means upon which realization of its professed aims depends. Liberalism can be true to its ideals only as it takes the course that leads to their attainment. The notion that organized social control of economic forces lies outside the historic path of liberalism shows that liberalism is still impeded by remnants of its earlier *laissez faire* phase, with its opposition of society and the individual. The thing which now dampens liberal ardor and paralyzes its efforts is the conception that liberty and development of individuality as ends exclude the use of organized social effort as means. Earlier liberalism regarded the separate and competing economic action of individuals as the means to social well-being as the end. We must reverse the perspective and see that socialized economy is the means of free individual development as the end.

That liberals are divided in outlook and endeavor while reactionaries are held together by community of interests and the ties of custom is well-nigh a commonplace. Organization of standpoint and belief among liberals can be achieved only in and by unity of endeavor. Organized unity of action attended by consensus of beliefs will come about in the degree in which social control of economic forces is made the goal of liberal action. The greatest educational power, the greatest force in shaping the dispositions and attitudes of individuals, is the social medium in which they live. The medium that now lies closest to us is that of unified action for the inclusive end of a social-ized economy. The attainment of a state of society in which a basis of material security will release the powers of individuals for cultural expression is not the work of a day. But by concen-trating upon the task of securing a socialized economy as the ground and medium for release of the impulses and capacities men agree to call ideal, the now scattered and often conflicting activities of liberals can be brought to effective unity.

It is no part of my task to outline in detail a program for renascent liberalism. But the question of "what is to be done" cannot be ignored. Ideas must be organized, and this organiza-tion implies an organization of individuals who hold these ideas and whose faith is ready to translate itself into action. Translation into action signifies that the general creed of lib-eralism be formulated as a concrete program of action. It is in organization for action that liberals are weak, and without this organization there is danger that democratic ideals may go by default. Democracy has been a fighting faith. When its ideals are reenforced by those of scientific method and experimental intelligence, it cannot be that it is incapable of evoking disci-pline, ardor and organization. To narrow the issue for the future to a struggle between Fascism and Communism is to invite a catastrophe that may carry civilization down in the struggle. Vital and courageous democratic liberalism is the one force that can surely avoid such a disastrous narrowing of the issue. I for one do not believe that Americans living in the tradition of Jefferson and Lincoln will weaken and give up without a whole-hearted effort to make democracy a living reality. This, I repeat, involves organization.

The question cannot be answered by argument. Experimental method means experiment, and the question can be answered only by trying, by organized effort. The reasons for making the trial are not abstract or recondite. They are found in the confusion, uncertainty and conflict that mark the modern world. The reasons for thinking that the effort if made will be successful are also not abstract and remote. They lie in what the method of experimental and cooperative intelligence has already accomplished in subduing to potential human use the energies of physical nature. In material production, the method of intelligence is now the established rule; to abandon it would be to revert to savagery. The task is to go on, and not backward, until the method of intelligence and experimental control is the rule in social relations and social direction. Either we take this road or we admit that the problem of social organization in behalf of human liberty and the flowering of human capacities is insoluble.

It would be fantastic folly to ignore or to belittle the obstacles that stand in the way. But what has taken place, also against great odds, in the scientific and industrial revolutions, is an accomplished fact; the way is marked out. It may be that the way will remain untrodden. If so, the future holds the menace of confusion moving into chaos, a chaos that will be externally masked for a time by an organization of force, coercive and violent, in which the liberties of men will all but disappear. Even so, the cause of the liberty of the human spirit, the cause of opportunity of human beings for full development of their powers, the cause for which liberalism enduringly stands, is too precious and too ingrained in the human constitution to be forever obscured. Intelligence after millions of years of errancy has found itself as a method, and it will not be lost forever in the blackness of night. The business of liberalism is to bend every energy and exhibit every courage so that these precious goods may not even be temporarily lost but be intensified and expanded here and now.

GREAT BOOKS IN PHILOSOPHY PAPERBACK SERIES

ESTHETICS

❑ Aristotle—*The Poetics*
❑ Aristotle—*Treatise on Rhetoric*

ETHICS

❑ Aristotle—*The Nicomachean Ethics*
❑ Marcus Aurelius—*Meditations*
❑ Jeremy Bentham—*The Principles of Morals and Legislation*
❑ John Dewey—*Human Nature and Conduct*
❑ John Dewey—*The Moral Writings of John Dewey, Revised Edition*
❑ Epictetus—*Enchiridion*
❑ David Hume—*An Enquiry Concerning the Principles of Morals*
❑ Immanuel Kant—*Fundamental Principles of the Metaphysic of Morals*
❑ John Stuart Mill—*Utilitarianism*
❑ George Edward Moore—*Principia Ethica*
❑ Friedrich Nietzsche—*Beyond Good and Evil*
❑ Plato—*Protagoras, Philebus, and Gorgias*
❑ Bertrand Russell—*Bertrand Russell On Ethics, Sex, and Marriage*
❑ Arthur Schopenhauer—*The Wisdom of Life* and *Counsels and Maxims*
❑ Adam Smith—*The Theory of Moral Sentiments*
❑ Benedict de Spinoza—*Ethics* and *The Improvement of the Understanding*

LOGIC

❑ George Boole—*The Laws of Thought*

METAPHYSICS/EPISTEMOLOGY

❑ Aristotle—*De Anima*
❑ Aristotle—*The Metaphysics*
❑ Francis Bacon—*Essays*
❑ George Berkeley—*Three Dialogues Between Hylas and Philonous*
❑ W. K. Clifford—*The Ethics of Belief and Other Essays*
❑ René Descartes—*Discourse on Method* and *The Meditations*
❑ John Dewey—*How We Think*
❑ John Dewey—*The Influence of Darwin on Philosophy and Other Essays*
❑ Epicurus—*The Essential Epicurus: Letters, Principal Doctrines,*
   Vatican Sayings, and Fragments
❑ Sidney Hook—*The Quest for Being*
❑ David Hume—*An Enquiry Concerning Human Understanding*
❑ David Hume—*A Treatise on Human Nature*
❑ William James—*The Meaning of Truth*
❑ William James—*Pragmatism*
❑ Immanuel Kant—*The Critique of Judgment*
❑ Immanuel Kant—*Critique of Practical Reason*
❑ Immanuel Kant—*Critique of Pure Reason*
❑ Gottfried Wilhelm Leibniz—*Discourse on Metaphysics* and *The Monadology*
❑ John Locke—*An Essay Concerning Human Understanding*
❑ George Herbert Mead—*The Philosophy of the Present*

- ❏ Michel de Montaigne—*Essays*
- ❏ Charles S. Peirce—*The Essential Writings*
- ❏ Plato—*The Euthyphro, Apology, Crito,* and *Phaedo*
- ❏ Plato—*Lysis, Phaedrus, and Symposium*
- ❏ Bertrand Russell—*The Problems of Philosophy*
- ❏ George Santayana—*The Life of Reason*
- ❏ Sextus Empiricus—*Outlines of Pyrrhonism*
- ❏ Ludwig Wittgenstein—*Wittgenstein's Lectures: Cambridge, 1932–1935*
- ❏ Alfred North Whitehead—*The Concept of Nature*

PHILOSOPHY OF RELIGION

- ❏ Jeremy Bentham—*The Influence of Natural Religion on the Temporal Happiness of Mankind*
- ❏ Marcus Tullius Cicero—*The Nature of the Gods* and *On Divination*
- ❏ Ludwig Feuerbach—*The Essence of Christianity*
- ❏ Paul Henri Thiry, Baron d'Holbach—*Good Sense*
- ❏ David Hume—*Dialogues Concerning Natural Religion*
- ❏ William James—*The Varieties of Religious Experience*
- ❏ John Locke—*A Letter Concerning Toleration*
- ❏ Lucretius—*On the Nature of Things*
- ❏ John Stuart Mill—*Three Essays on Religion*
- ❏ Friedrich Nietzsche—*The Antichrist*
- ❏ Thomas Paine—*The Age of Reason*
- ❏ Bertrand Russell—*Bertrand Russell On God and Religion*

SOCIAL AND POLITICAL PHILOSOPHY

- ❏ Aristotle—*The Politics*
- ❏ Mikhail Bakunin—*The Basic Bakunin: Writings, 1869–1871*
- ❏ Edmund Burke—*Reflections on the Revolution in France*
- ❏ John Dewey—*Freedom and Culture*
- ❏ John Dewey—*Individualism Old and New*
- ❏ John Dewey—*Liberalism and Social Action*
- ❏ G. W. F. Hegel—*The Philosophy of History*
- ❏ G. W. F. Hegel—*Philosophy of Right*
- ❏ Thomas Hobbes—*The Leviathan*
- ❏ Sidney Hook—*Paradoxes of Freedom*
- ❏ Sidney Hook—*Reason, Social Myths, and Democracy*
- ❏ John Locke—*The Second Treatise on Civil Government*
- ❏ Niccolo Machiavelli—*The Prince*
- ❏ Karl Marx (with Friedrich Engels)—*The Economic and Philosophic Manuscripts of 1844* and *The Communist Manifesto*
- ❏ Karl Marx (with Friedrich Engels)—*The German Ideology,* including *Theses on Feuerbach* and *Introduction to the Critique of Political Economy*
- ❏ Karl Marx—*The Poverty of Philosophy*
- ❏ John Stuart Mill—*Considerations on Representative Government*
- ❏ John Stuart Mill—*On Liberty*
- ❏ John Stuart Mill—*On Socialism*
- ❏ John Stuart Mill—*The Subjection of Women*

- ❏ Montesquieu, Charles de Secondat—*The Spirit of Laws*
- ❏ Friedrich Nietzsche—*Thus Spake Zarathustra*
- ❏ Thomas Paine—*Common Sense*
- ❏ Thomas Paine—*Rights of Man*
- ❏ Plato—*Laws*
- ❏ Plato—*The Republic*
- ❏ Jean-Jacques Rousseau—*Émile*
- ❏ Jean-Jacques Rousseau—*The Social Contract*
- ❏ Mary Wollstonecraft—*A Vindication of the Rights of Men*
- ❏ Mary Wollstonecraft—*A Vindication of the Rights of Women*

GREAT MINDS PAPERBACK SERIES

ART

- ❏ Leonardo da Vinci—*A Treatise on Painting*

ECONOMICS

- ❏ Charlotte Perkins Gilman—*Women and Economics: A Study of the Economic Relation between Women and Men*
- ❏ John Maynard Keynes—*The End of Laissez Faire* and *The Economic Consequences of the Peace*
- ❏ John Maynard Keynes—*The General Theory of Employment, Interest, and Money*
- ❏ John Maynard Keynes—*A Tract on Monetary Reform*
- ❏ Thomas R. Malthus—*An Essay on the Principle of Population*
- ❏ Alfred Marshall—*Money, Credit, and Commerce*
- ❏ Alfred Marshall—*Principles of Economics*
- ❏ Karl Marx—*Theories of Surplus Value*
- ❏ John Stuart Mill—*Principles of Political Economy*
- ❏ David Ricardo—*Principles of Political Economy and Taxation*
- ❏ Adam Smith—*Wealth of Nations*
- ❏ Thorstein Veblen—*Theory of the Leisure Class*

HISTORY

- ❏ Edward Gibbon—*On Christianity*
- ❏ Alexander Hamilton, John Jay, and James Madison—*The Federalist*
- ❏ Herodotus—*The History*
- ❏ Charles Mackay—*Extraordinary Popular Delusions and the Madness of Crowds*
- ❏ Thucydides—*History of the Peloponnesian War*

LAW

- ❏ John Austin—*The Province of Jurisprudence Determined*

LITERATURE

- ❏ Jonathan Swift—*A Modest Proposal and Other Satires*
- ❏ H. G. Wells—*The Conquest of Time*

PSYCHOLOGY

❏ Sigmund Freud—*Totem and Taboo*

RELIGION/FREETHOUGHT

❏ Desiderius Erasmus—*The Praise of Folly*
❏ Thomas Henry Huxley—*Agnosticism and Christianity and Other Essays*
❏ Ernest Renan—*The Life of Jesus*
❏ Upton Sinclair—*The Profits of Religion*
❏ Elizabeth Cady Stanton—*The Woman's Bible*
❏ Voltaire—*A Treatise on Toleration and Other Essays*
❏ Andrew D. White—*A History of the Warfare of Science with Theology in Christendom*

SCIENCE

❏ Jacob Bronowski—*The Identity of Man*
❏ Nicolaus Copernicus—*On the Revolutions of Heavenly Spheres*
❏ Marie Curie—*Radioactive Substances*
❏ Charles Darwin—*The Autobiography of Charles Darwin*
❏ Charles Darwin—*The Descent of Man*
❏ Charles Darwin—*The Origin of Species*
❏ Charles Darwin—*The Voyage of the Beagle*
❏ René Descartes—*Treatise of Man*
❏ Albert Einstein—*Relativity*
❏ Michael Faraday—*The Forces of Matter*
❏ Galileo Galilei—*Dialogues Concerning Two New Sciences*
❏ Ernst Haeckel—*The Riddle of the Universe*
❏ William Harvey—*On the Motion of the Heart and Blood in Animals*
❏ Werner Heisenberg—*Physics and Philosophy*
❏ Julian Huxley—*Evolutionary Humanism*
❏ Thomas H. Huxley—*Evolution and Ethics* and *Science and Morals*
❏ Edward Jenner—*Vaccination against Smallpox*
❏ Johannes Kepler—*Epitome of Copernican Astronomy* and *Harmonies of the World*
❏ James Clerk Maxwell—*Matter and Motion*
❏ Isaac Newton—*Opticks, Or Treatise of the Reflections, Inflections, and Colours of Light*
❏ Isaac Newton—*The Principia*
❏ Louis Pasteur and Joseph Lister—*Germ Theory and Its Application to Medicine* and *On the Antiseptic Principle of the Practice of Surgery*
❏ William Thomson (Lord Kelvin) and Peter Guthrie Tait—*The Elements of Natural Philosophy*
❏ Alfred Russel Wallace—*Island Life*

SOCIOLOGY

❏ Emile Durkheim—*Ethics and the Sociology of Morals*